RISE
of the
CHAMPIONS

TONY MELVIN

Rise of the Champions

Published by
Tony Melvin
tonymelvin.com

Copyright © 2019 Tony Melvin
All Rights Reserved.

Cover design by Tony Melvin.

MetaPulse is a Trademark of exec.io and is used with permission.

No part of this book may be reproduced without the permission of the copyright owner.

Disclaimers

The author and publisher expressly disclaim all and any liability to any person, whether a purchaser of this publication or not, in respect of anything and of the consequences of anything done or omitted to be done by any such person in reliance, whether whole or partial, upon the whole or any part of the contents of this publication.

This is a work of fiction. Names, characters, businesses, places, events, locales, and incidents are either the products of the author's imagination or used in a fictitious manner. Any resemblance to actual persons, living or dead, or actual events is purely coincidental.

Contents

WEEK 1	1
WEEK 2	7
WEEK 3	20
WEEK 4	27
WEEK 5	35
WEEK 6	43
WEEK 7	59
WEEK 8	68
WEEK 20 (3 months later)	71
WEEK 24 (4 weeks later)	76
WEEK 28 (4 weeks later)	77
WEEK 32 (4 weeks later)	79
WEEK 52	83
WEEK 54	86
A Final Word, from Tony	89

Also by Tony Melvin

Rich Habits

Market Genius

TRUE TEAM

*To my late mother
who often reminded me, while growing up,
"You can do anything."
Thanks, Mam. I miss you.*

WEEK 1

The wrench slipped from my grip and I hit my hand hard on the metal frame.

"ARRGGGGG," I screamed.

I picked up the wrench and threw it across the factory floor.

"GODDAM FLUFFY-DUCK."

I kicked an empty cardboard box, hard. Only it wasn't empty. It was jam-packed with thick paper, which means it was like kicking a rock.

"MOTHER FLUFFY-DUCK," I yelled.

In case you haven't noticed, I was mad. Really mad. I looked around the factory to see what else I could kick (that was soft). I hated this place. I hated every piece of machinery. I hated the smell. I hated everything. Most of all, I hated the fact that it was Friday night, close to midnight and I was stuck here working. What makes that fact even more depressing is that I am the boss. I own this God-forsaken joint. Yeah, that's right—I'm an "entrepreneur," and I hate it.

I should also explain the "fluffy-duck." You see, my wife doesn't like me swearing. She made me promise that I would always use a different word—one that sounds so stupid that I'd refrain from using it in public. She chose the word and it works. Now I only employ my custom profanity while alone. Like now. The rest of the time I say things like, "Oh, darn it."

Breathing heavily, in varying degrees of physical pain, I glanced up at the wall and saw his face: Nelson Mandela. He is the only thing I cannot hate, no matter how mad I am. I read the quote under the photo, although I knew it by heart. Afterall, I had put it there.

> *The greatest glory in living lies not in never falling,
> but in rising every time we fall.*

There are two things that make me snap out of a bad mood. One is that quote, knowing whatever I'm going through, Nelson Mandela went through worse. The other is pretty much any song by *Queen*, especially *We Are the Champions*.

OK, it was time to rise and it was time for some *Queen*. It was also time for pizza, because I realized I'd skipped dinner trying to get this job done. That's another thing I've noticed: lack of sleep and food is the perfect recipe for a bad mood.

I walked to my office and fired up my computer. I'm sad to say that the local pizza joint knows me well. I ordered my pre-saved usual with just a few clicks. Now it was time to call the wife and give her the bad news. I glanced at the family photo sitting on my desk amongst the messy paperwork; it was a beautiful shot of me and Tiffany with the kids, taken about 3 years ago. We've been married twelve... no, make that thirteen years. I know because my son Tim will be twelve this year and Jessica will be ten. Where have the years gone? Especially the last five. Ever since I became my own boss, I've hardly seen them. And here I go again, calling late to tell her I'm not coming home.

She picked up on the first ring. "Hi honey, it's me," I said.

"On your way home?" she asked.

I paused. Hardly a second but she knew. "Oh John, not again? It's Timmy's baseball game in the morning!"

"Don't worry, I'll be there. The damn printing machine jammed again so I have to fix it before I can continue."

"You can't keep doing this John. We hardly ever see you and it's not healthy. You're there all day and practically all night."

"I know honey but I've got to pay the bills somehow."

"You made more money in your old job and we got to *see* you," she pleaded, stretching out that word "see" for added effect.

It wasn't the first time we had this conversation. She knew this was my dream, to be my own boss and to build a big business. But five years of long hours and little reward was taking its toll. She'd never say it outright, knowing the idea would be the end of my dream, but it was implied and I knew what she was thinking: *Just sell the damn business and let's have a normal life.* Truth is, I'd thought of it too. Problem is, the debt we were carrying was more than the business was worth. I was, to be blunt, trapped.

"Tiffany I know. Look, I better get cracking. Love you."

"Love you too."

I hung up. Now I really needed some *Queen*. The one thing I had done, because I was the boss and I could, was install big speakers around the factory. I opened my favourite playlists, all *Queen* songs, arranged in such a way that *We Are the Champions* repeated every fourth or fifth song. It was also the first. I clicked play and cranked the volume.

Freddie belted out the first few lyrics.

I'm not sure exactly who Freddie Mercury wrote this song for, but in my opinion, it's perfect for the business owner, the struggling entrepreneur. It's perfect for people like me.

I sang along. Those lyrics about "mistakes" were certainly written for me. Although, I'd made more than a few.

I heard the doorbell buzz just barely above the music. Dinner!

I tipped the pizza guy a buck. Bit stingy I know, but the kid probably earned more than me. The smell of the pizza lifted my spirits. I joined Freddie in the fourth verse at the top of my lungs and sang along.

I am not going to lose.

I bought this business 5 years ago. I had to borrow money. I mortgaged the house but was still short. My folks came to the rescue, my dad saying, "We believe in you son."

It was a printing business. We printed stuff: flyers, postcards, posters, menus, you name it, we could do it. I called it *Champion Printing Services*. No prizes knowing where that name came from. Our slogan was corny as hell: *Your first choice for all your printing needs.* And our unique selling position, which was something a marketing guru told me we had to have was *Guaranteed on-time delivery or it's free.*

That's why I'm here on a Friday at midnight. This printing job was due by 12pm tomorrow. Why anyone had a deadline for 12pm on a Saturday was beyond me. The problem wasn't so much the deadline but the price. This was a big job, about $20,000 worth of printing. One of our biggest, sold by my star sales guy Richard. However, the profit margin was pathetic. But this was part of Richard's plan to break into the wholesale market. He was undercutting the competition to get his foot in the door. Due to the size of these wholesale jobs we did them mostly at night, because Betty (that's what we call the large 4-stage printing machine, our biggest) needed to run all night. Drew, our lead technician and a great bloke, did the smaller jobs during the day.

With such tight margins I couldn't afford to pay the overtime rates. So I of course had to do the jobs because, you know, I'm willing to work for nothing.

With food in my belly and *Queen* bellowing around the factory, I looked at Betty. She was like a Model T Ford, not a single computer chip inside her. She was old, somewhat reliable, but easy to repair.

"Right, let's get you fixed," I said to her. "I've got a baseball game in less than 10 hours that I'm not going to miss."

The first problem was, where the hell had I thrown that wrench?

Around 6 a.m. I stifled a yawn. Betty was pumping away rhythmically. Strange how it's possible to feel drowsy with such a loud noise. I could lie down next to her and fall asleep right now. Concrete floor and all.

Time for coffee.

I made it strong and sat back, checking the time against Betty's progress; we were on target. I could be out of here by 9am and make the game.

I wandered back to my office and picked up a business magazine off my desk. I get these mailed to me every month. I'm always looking for tips on how to improve things; marketing, systems, recruitment, anything. Mostly all I find is the same stuff repeated: expensive seminars or online courses with buzzwords and clichés. Maybe I'm cynical, but still I keep looking, hoping to find the holy grail for business.

Flicking through the mag, I noticed an article with the headline:

From zero to $100 Million in 10 Years

Whow! That's huge growth. My headline would read: $500,000 to zero in 5 years. Anyway, the article sucked me in. I started to read. There was a picture of a guy smiling, wearing a suit that looked like it cost more than my car. The subtitle said his name was Mike Salsburg. Hey, I knew a Mike Salsburg. I continued reading. Mike started a freight company ten years ago and worked himself to the bone, with late hours, tough clients and little profit. Ha, I thought, I'm on the right path. But then he changed his operating basis completely; through trial and error, he developed ten key business principles that turned everything around. Within two years he had hit $10M, then $20M, then $40M and through acquisitions and stellar organic growth, he jumped to $60M and then $100M. This line got me, "And I did it all without sacrificing what's important: family, friends and fun."

I wanted to know if this guy had written a book or something. What were those ten principles he mentioned? I read the little bio next to his photo. "With no college education, Mike learned business from the ground up, after his parents moved from Central City."

I couldn't believe it; that's where I lived. This was my old friend Mike. We were best buddies in the sixth grade. I could see it now in his photo; he had the same cheeky smile. He had introduced me to *Queen*. We used to sing along to every song. I'd play air guitar and Mike would play air drums. We'd both play air piano. I felt a wave of nostalgia wash over me. I cried when he left (don't tell anyone). And look at him now! My old buddy Mike was truly kicking ass. And rich.

I wondered if he'd help me? He was probably too busy. I picked up my coffee mug and walked out into the factory reading the article all over again.

An energy welled up inside me. I felt a buzz. It wasn't the coffee; this coffee was so cheap it probably didn't even have any caffeine. I wondered if this was perhaps my lucky break? Would Mike be willing to help an old friend?

I looked up at Mandela. "What do you think?"

He seemed to smile at me. I think I even heard him say, "It's time to rise."

WEEK 2

The weekend couldn't be over quick enough. I couldn't stop thinking about Mike. I googled him to find out more about him and his company. Amazing story.

The baseball game went well; I managed to stay awake. On Sunday, despite feeling exhausted, I was back in my office doing the job I hated the most: finances— working out how much money I didn't have. I worked out what bills we could pay and what we couldn't. The latter was always the longer list. It was depressing.

I read Mike's article again and wondered what he was doing today. Probably on a million-dollar yacht with a butler named Alfred. Lucky fluffy-duck. Despite my pitiful situation, I was feeling a sense of hope. Maybe Mike would help me? I wasn't interested in a yacht or a butler; I'd just like to spend my weekends with my family.

∽

I rolled through the office door just after 8 a.m. Monday morning.
"Morning Sally."
"Good morning John. Have a good weekend?"
Sally was my loyal receptionist, office manager and general life saver. She'd been here longer than me and was one of two employees who came with the business when I bought it. Joe, a salesman, was the other. Sally was probably in her late fifties. Never had a day off sick, always chirpy and bubbly. Great with clients, but tough as nails when it came to collections. She always wore pink.
"The usual and you?" I asked.

"We had trivia night on Saturday with the local bowls club ladies."

"Oh, why wasn't I invited?"

"You're too young John and you are not a lady. Besides, you need to spend more time with your family."

Despite being only a decade older than me, Sally acted more like my surrogate mother than my employee. I think if I ever tried to fire her she'd tell me off and send me to my room.

I eyed her curiously. "Have you been speaking to my wife?"

Sally and my wife worked as cohorts to get me out of the office and plan my schedule. Often I'd call Tiffany to tell her I'd be missing dinner and she'd just answer the phone with, "I know, Sally told me."

Sally replied, with that mother-knows-everything look. "More than you know John."

I gave her a "humph" in protest and pushed through the swinging doors to the factory.

Drew was already there working away next to Betty-the-printer with Steve and Todd, our young apprenticing technicians, manning the other smaller machines. I gave them a wave. Joe and Richard would be in later after they made their Monday morning sales calls.

I went to my office, sat down at my desk, eager to make my most important call of the day to *Salsburg Freight*. Over the weekend I'd found the phone number for the head office. I dialed it eagerly.

"Salsburg Freight, how may I direct your call?" said a pretty voice who I think was probably half the age of Sally.

"Er ... hi," I mumbled." Er... I'm an old friend of Mike's, er Mike Freight, I mean Mike Salsburg. We went to school together; anyway, I guess he's busy but I just wanted to leave a message."

"Certainly, may I have your full name and best contact number?" she said without missing a beat. Very professional. I expected her to hang up.

I gave her my details and she politely said she'd pass on the message. Now all I had to do was wait.

I hate waiting. I needed to keep busy.

Joe arrived shortly after nine. He walked in, as he did everyday, looking the same. He was wearing the same white shirt, carrying the same briefcase, with the same pens stuffed in his shirt pocket, with our logo on it. "Morning Joe," I said.

"Morning John. Good weekend?"

"The usual and you?"

He just nodded.

Joe was a man of few words. How he ever sold anything, I'd never know. He wasn't stellar, but he was reliable. Week in, week out, he brought in the orders. Not big orders, but steady. Mostly small. He had three kids in college, was a little overweight and balding. Like Sally, he never had a sick day, but unlike Sally, he never wore pink. Always the same white shirt, pocket pens and briefcase.

"Close any deals?" This phrase was the extent of my sales management expertise with Joe. It's all I ever asked him, aside from "how was your weekend?"

"Yes, several new business startup packages and a few re-orders," he said as he unpacked his briefcase with the signed orders.

Joe had a knack for finding new businesses in the area and contacting them before anyone else did. He'd sell them his startup packages of business cards, letterheads, flyers—that kind of thing. He'd even organize for a logo design if they didn't have one. They were usually about $1,000 worth of printing, often more, with pretty good profit margins too. And he would always call back, hand deliver the goods and get another order; he called those his re-orders.

But for a while now he hadn't brought in any big orders. He was always getting undercut by the competition.

"Great," I said. And that was it. I strolled back to my office.

Richard came in around ten, always later than Joe. He was my star. I hired him just over a year ago. He always looked impeccable. Business suit, red tie, slick hair, gold watch, black shiny shoes to match his slick hair. Richard was my man. "Hey Richard!" I yelled with enthusiasm.

He walked over to me bearing his big white smile and we high-fived and did the buddy handshake with a pat on the back. "What ya working on?" That was my sales management phrase for Richard.

"A big deal!" he said with a smile.

I loved it when he said that.

"About $80k," he beamed.

"Wow." That was nearly four times our biggest job ever. "Who is it?"

"It's a surprise!" he laughed.

We always played this game. He'd tell me about these big deals and I'd asked who, but he wouldn't tell me until the deal was done. Aside from it being a surprise, he said it was bad luck. I didn't want to test his luck, so I let him be.

I'd hired Richard because I wanted to get into the big time. I really wanted to boom this business. Joe was good and reliable, but he never brought in big deals. Richard, on the other hand, oozed with that big-deal vibe. He also told me that such deals take time, that getting people to spend big chunks of money took longer. It required more relationship building. I remember in his interview he told me, "John, to do big deals you need to have the patience of Mother Teresa, but the tenacity of Mike Tyson. And John, I have both." He said it with such intensity, looking me straight in the eyes, that I hired him on the spot. I often joked with him since, that he was Mother Tyson.

Sally's voice came over the speaker. "John call line two, some guy called Mike, won't say where from."

My stomach did a somersault. "Gotta go Richard." We bumped fists and I left.

I shut my office door, which I don't usually do and quickly moved to my desk, picking up the phone as I did.

"Hi Mike."

"Jonnie, is that you, Jonnie Maine?" Mike's voice was loud and boisterous.

"Yeah," I laughed.

"Oh buddy, how are you? Wow, it's been what? Thirty years?"

"Yeah, you're right about that. Well I'm good. Married. Two kids."

"Congratulations. I did it the other way: two wives, one kid."

I laughed. "Congratulations on your success. I read the article in the business mag."

"Thanks buddy. Lots of hard work, but fun. What are you doing with yourself?"

"I own my own business, but it's small of course."

"Good for you. What is it?"

"Printing. After school I did my apprenticeship and then five years ago I bought this business."

"Printing hey? Great business, always in demand. Is it going well?"

"Well, it's OK. Ups and downs, you know—like you said in your article."

"Yeah, it can be tough. Well, if you need any help, you let me know."

"Well, Mike, aside from wanting to say hello, I was hoping you might be able to help me."

"Sure buddy, what do you need? Looking for capital?"

"Oh no, nothing like that. What I really want to know is …" I sighed. I realized I didn't really know what I needed help with.

"You there Jonnie?"

"Yeah, sorry Mike," I sat down in my chair.

"What's up buddy?"

"Well, the truth is, I'm not sure. I'm working 80-plus hours a week, I hardly see the family and I barely break even." I sighed again. I hadn't said a word of this to anyone and suddenly I felt this wave of stress come over me. "I'm not sure how to get out of this rut Mike. I worked less and made more money when I was an employee."

"Yeah, I know. I know. Been there. Listen," then he said the most beautiful words this stressed-out, underpaid and overworked entrepreneur ever heard, "I can help you."

I was suddenly speechless. Something caught in my throat and my eyes got wet. Must be dust in this place.

"Jonnie?"

"Thanks Mike, that would be great," I croaked.

"Hey remember the song, *'You're My Best Friend'*?"

I had to wipe my eyes. "Yeah."

"Still applies," he said.

I think Mike tried to lighten the mood because he said, "Remember those days head-banging to *Queen* in my bedroom? Mom used to go berserk. That was fun."

I smiled through my tears and sniffed.

He continued, "OK, so I've got to go. I've got a meeting, but here's what we're going to do. I'll call you tomorrow at 8 a.m. Block out an hour. I want you to have two clean unused notebooks. OK?"

"Yeah, got it—8 a.m., two notebooks."

"Great, OK we'll talk then. So good to hear from you buddy."

"You too. Thanks Mike."

I hung up. I felt like a complete dimwit. But at the same time I felt a sense of relief. I must have bottled up a lot of stress because I'd never reacted that way. Never.

God, it was so good to talk to Mike.

I was at the office early, before anyone else. I had my two notebooks and several pens. I even organized my desk, so it was free of the usual clutter of paperwork. Well, "organized" is not entirely true; I just moved the mess into the drawer.

Drew showed up and popped his head in the office. "In early boss or did you never leave?"

"In early!" I said cheerfully.

He nodded with a smile. "I'm going to fix me a cuppa. Want one?"

"All good thanks," I said raising my mug.

He nodded again and headed off to the kitchen.

It was 7.30am. I still had some time to kill so I checked my emails.

At 8:01 the phone buzzed. I'd left a post-it note on Sally's computer screen to put Mike's call directly through.

"Morning John. Mike for you."

"Thanks Sally." The call switched over. "Mike," I said.

"Jonnie, how are you?"

"Doing great. Hey Mike, thanks again for your time. I really appreciate it."

"Pleasure buddy. OK, so tell me about your business, staff, sales, income, everything."

I gave him the "company tour" and laid it all on the line. He asked me pointed questions like, what was my turnover last year? How many sales did I make last week? How much did each sales guy make? How much did I make on each job? Every time I gave him a number he'd say, "Is that exact or an estimate?"

"Estimate," I'd reply.

After about 30 minutes of interrogation he said, "OK, I've heard enough."

I felt like he was going to tell me I was not fit for business and I should sell out quick before I went bankrupt. Instead he said, "You're in the exact same place I was in; it's the same place most business owners find themselves."

"Really?" I asked, shocked.

"Yep. Bad news is, it's going to take hard work to get out of it. Good news is, I know exactly how to help you do it."

"I'm not afraid of hard work Mike, but," I paused, "you probably already know, I don't have any money to pay you."

"We played air guitar together Jonnie. I don't charge my fellow band members for advice," he said.

"Mike, I'd have to give you something in return for your help."

"You will and it's called winning. Here's the deal Jonnie. We'll do a phone meeting once a week, every Tuesday at 8 a.m. I'll give you one key business principle at a time. Once you've mastered it we'll go on to the next. Each week you'll have action items you need to get done before the next meeting. I'm your friend Jonnie, but I won't go easy on you. Deal?"

"Deal, Mike."

"Good. Before I give you the first business principle take one of those notebooks. Label one *Business Principles;* label the other *Successful Actions*. Whenever I give you a business principle, write it on a new page in the notebook. As you implement it, keep a journal of what happens. When you get a successful action that works, write that down in the *Successful Actions* book. Make sense?"

"Yes." I scribbled these instructions on the front page of my open notebook.

"Great, now business is like climbing stairs. You get your way to the top by taking each step at a time. And here's the first principle: Always measure the important steps towards your desired outcome."

I wrote it down on a new page in my notebook.

Always measure the important
steps towards your desired outcome.

"For example, your goal in business is to make a profit, right?" he asked.

"Er... yeah," I said, unsure.

"Well, if you don't make a profit you won't survive. Some people think wanting to make a profit is greedy. That's nonsense. Profit means survival. Ripping people off, that's greedy. Providing great service and products at a profit, that's business; it means secure jobs, a working economy and taxes for the government, which means schools, roads, hospitals, etc. None of that can happen without profit. So, you want to make a profit; that's at the top of the stairs."

"Agreed."

"Good, so how do you make a profit?"

"I provide quality printing services at affordable—"

He cut me off. "Stop there. You provide quality printing services. Good, now before you provide it, what do you have to do?"

"Er ... sell it?"

"After that?" he asked.

"Print it?"

"And after you print it?"

"Deliver it?" I said.

"Correct. So, your stairway to profit consists of sales, getting the job printed and then delivery, right?"

"Yes."

"What do you have to do before you sell?"

"Provide a quote?" I guessed.

"Good, are you writing this down?"

"I am now."

"From the top down: profit, delivery, jobs printed, sales, quotes. What's next?"

"Leads or prospects?"

"What about appointments? Before your guys sell they first need to make a sales call."

"Oh, yeah." I scribbled out my mistake and added appointments.

"Then leads and what's next? What do you do to get leads?"

I was thinking, but Mike jumped in.

"Promotion— you must *always* promote."

I wrote it down.

"Now, read the list back to me from the top."

I read Mike my list:

Profit
Delivery
Jobs Printed
Sales
Quotes
Appointments
Leads
Promotion

"Good," Mike said. "There is one missing step and that is income. Before you can make a profit you need income, so add that between profit and delivery."

I rewrote the list.

>Profit
>Income
>Delivery
>Jobs Printed
>Sales
>Quotes
>Appointments
>Leads
>Promotion

Mike continued. "Now you apply the first principle. You need to measure each step. Collect them every day and tally them at the end of the week. You want to know exactly how many appointments were done each day; how many leads and quotes; how many jobs got delivered and so on. Understood?"

"Yeah, but how do I measure promotion?" I asked.

"How many promotional pieces were sent out, such as emails, flyers, ads, whatever," he said.

"I know that one is zero at the moment," I confessed.

"No surprise; we'll fix that," he said. "You need to put in a system to start collecting these stats. Once the system is in place, get someone you can trust to follow up the team and get it done."

"So, I just collect these numbers every day?"

"Yes, we're going to put these on a line graph. No fancy pie charts or anything else. Just line graphs, where up equals good and down equals bad. You'll start to see if your business is getting better or worse. We'll be able to spot exactly where the trouble is."

"Genius," I said.

"Oh, I almost forgot. Write down this website: metapulse.com. That's the stats system you'll use. It's easy and will provide the graphs you need and it's free to start with. Once you setup your team they will enter their stats directly into that system."

"OK cool." I already felt like this alone could turn my business around. "Anything else?" I asked.

"No that's it. That's your assignment for this week. Once you've got your team reporting daily, see if you can get the stats together for the prior 3 months, at least for the sales and above."

"OK, will do."

"Good. OK, I gotta fly. Talk next week."

"Hey Mike, thanks again. I already feel like this will make a huge difference."

"It will; it's the key to success. If you want to improve something, you first need to measure it. Gotta go, see ya."

Priceless. I wrote that last line in my notebook too.

Now it was time to get busy.

I wrote up an explanation for each of the "important steps" and assigned them to different team members as follows:

Profit - Sally
Income - Sally
Delivery - Sally
Jobs Printed - Drew
Sales - Richard & Joe
Quotes - Richard & Joe
Appointments - Richard & Joe
Leads - Sally
Promotion - Sally

I called an office meeting with the team. I told them about Mike, my old pal and showed them his article. Richard asked if he could keep the magazine, but I told him to get his own copy. Next to my *Queen* albums and my pictures of Mandela, that was my new prized possession.

I then explained that business was like climbing stairs and I showed them our simple stairway, from promotion to profit.

"Now, what we're going to do is measure these steps every day." I felt so pumped. "Sally, seeing as you do the bookkeeping and schedule deliveries, I need you to start tracking those. Also track any new leads that come through. Plus, we'll start sending out promotion and I'll get you to track that."

"OK," she said. "I'll do up a spreadsheet to track them."

"That would be great. There's an online app we'll be using that Mike recommends, but for now, use the spreadsheet."

Next, I turned to Drew. "Drew, I want you to track the number of printed jobs done each day. By done I mean completed so it's ready for delivery. Make sense?"

"Sure, no problem. How should I report it?" he asked.

"You can tell me and I'll put it in the spreadsheet for you," offered Sally.

"Perfect," I agreed. Gee, I loved my team. "Richard and Joe, I want you both to track your individual sales, quotes and appointments."

"Should we send them to Sally?" Joe asked.

I looked at Sally.

"Yes, we may as well put it all in the spreadsheet," she said.

"Great. Any questions?" I asked.

Richard leaned forward with a frown. "You want us to report this every day?"

"Yes," I said.

"But some days sales will be zero. Seems a bit pointless to track them daily; why not track them monthly? That's what most professional businesses do." he said.

"Well, Mike said do it daily and I'm following his advice," I said.

"Yeah, but his business is different. He's in the freight industry; they have activity going on every day. We're only a small business. Seems like a lot of extra work for no point," he said.

I was surprised. Out of all the people on the team, Richard was the least enthusiastic. "Well I want …"

He cut me off. "John, you know I work on big deals that take longer. How about I report once a month instead?"

He had a point. I wish I could ask Mike.

"How about the first of every month?" he offered.

"OK," I relented. "You do the first of each month. Joe, are you OK doing it daily or do you want to do it each month?"

"Daily is fine with me," Joe said.

"Great, thanks team. So we start today." Then I had a thought. "Actually, if you can all remember what you did yesterday, report it to Sally. And Richard, you report what you did last month."

They all nodded, except Richard, who was looking at his phone.

"Great. Well, that's all unless there are any other questions?"

Everyone shook their heads.

Business principle number one was underway. I made a note in my journal, under the principle, to summarise the meeting. I felt a new sense of pride I hadn't felt since I first purchased the business. We were going to start climbing the steps to profit.

WEEK 3

I was at my desk early. It was Tuesday and I had my weekly call with Mike. Over the past week the daily reporting of the "steps" slowly sank in. Sometimes people forgot to do their part, but Sally said the daily stats had to be reported by 9am the following day or else. Of course, we all complied.

I also checked out that online app Mike recommended called MetaPulse. I played around and created graphs for each of the "stairways to profit," including graphs for Richard and Joe. I also found a cool feature that allows you to add the graphs together, so the total sales, for example, was a total of Richard's and Joe's sales.

When I showed Sally, she got all excited and immediately added the numbers she'd collected from the team. I had the app open on my screen and for the first time ever I could see the activity of my business. Here's what the daily activity for the past week looked like:

RISE OF THE CHAMPIONS

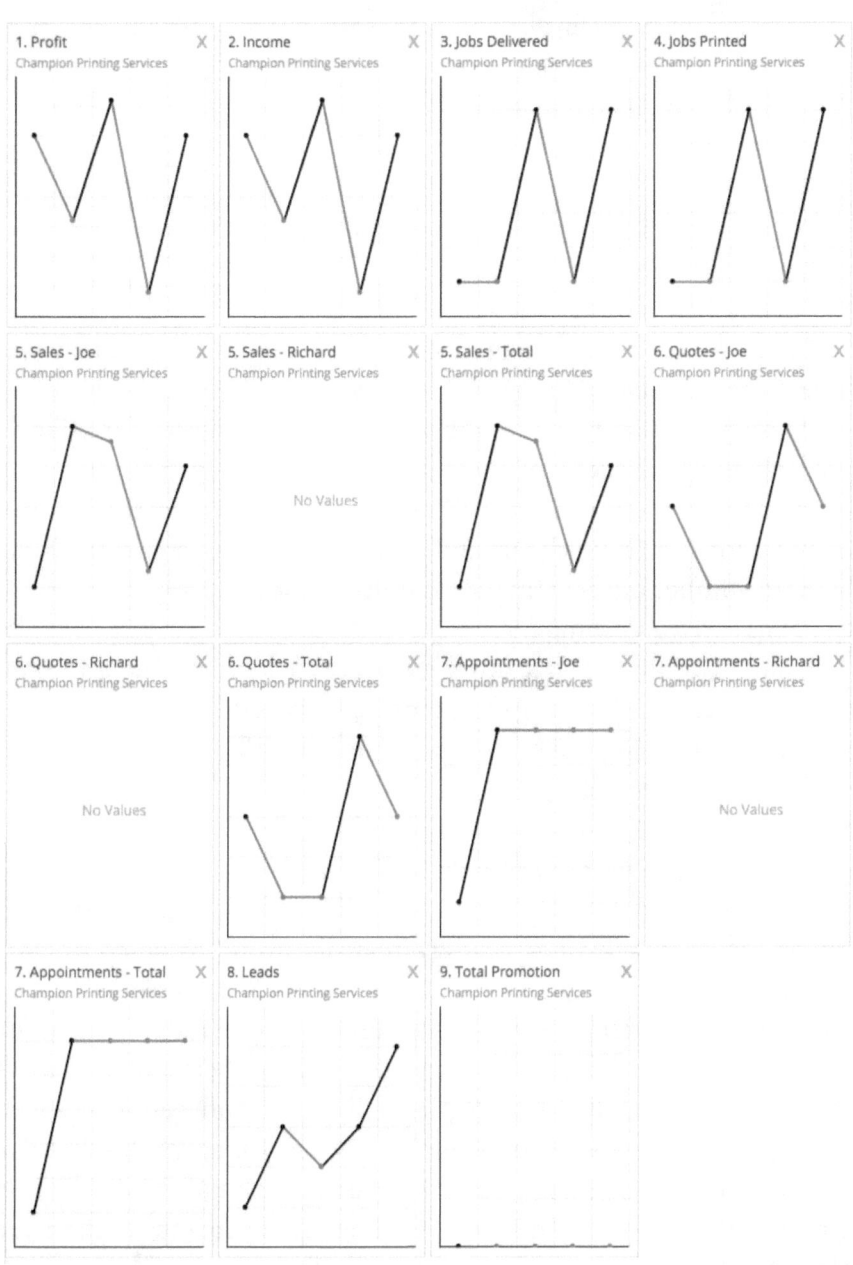

At 8am my phone buzzed. "Mike for you John," said Sally.

"Mike!" I said with excitement, like a child with an ice cream.

"Jonnie, how was your week?"

"Brilliant. I'm looking at the stairway to profit, with each graph on my screen."

"Great work. So no problems with the team?"

"No, everyone loves the idea."

"Really?" he said, surprised.

"Yeah! Well, Richard, my top sales guy, thought doing it daily was excessive so he's going to report monthly instead."

There was a brief pause on the line, which was unusual for Mike. "I see. Tell me about Richard," he said.

I raved on about how great Richard was: his style, dress, his idea of going for wholesale clients and building up massive volume. Mike listened without interrupting. Also unusual for Mike.

"What are you paying him?"

"A lot," I confessed. "He costs me over one hundred thousand per year, plus benefits, like fuel allowance, medical, etc."

"I see. I guess he's out of the office most days?"

"Yeah, on sales calls."

"How do you know?" he asked bluntly.

"Well … er … well, that's what he tells me."

"Jonnie, if he's making daily sales calls then he can damn well report his stats daily." I sensed an intensity in Mike's voice I hadn't heard before. It wasn't anger, but it was a kind of ruthlessness. "There are three types of people in business: the champions, the losers and the champion killers. The champions work hard, do their job and report their stats. Thankfully, most people are like that. Some are losers who don't produce enough to warrant their pay. They are parasites who live off the hard work of others. Then there are the champion killers; these guys are like vampires. They suck the life out of you and when you're almost dead, they help put the final nail in the coffin."

I gulped. I'd never heard Mike talk like this. "You sound like you're talking from experience?"

"You bet. I've had my fair share of vampires."

"But you're not suggesting that Richard is..."

"No, I'm not, but the stats will tell. In my experience, the only ones who ever balk and kick up a fuss about reporting their daily stats are either losers or vampires. Occasionally, a highly-productive person will see it as a distraction from doing their job, but once they see the benefits of monitoring their own performance, they become zealots on the subject." He paused. "You need to tell Richard that it's company policy; he needs to report daily. You want to know what activity is occurring daily so you can tally it weekly. You want to know this week is better and more productive than last week. If it isn't better, then you can fix it fast so next week is better. Waiting a month is too slow."

"OK," I said. I was not looking forward to telling Richard.

"Good, now let's move on to the next principle. You ready?"

"Yep." I had my notebook open, but I had already scribbled a bunch of notes from the conversation, so I turned to a new page.

"Business is like a thermometer," Mike said.

"I thought you said it was like climbing steps?" I interrupted.

"That was last week."

"OK."

"Business is like a thermometer. You need to know what the temperature is; otherwise you can die. Like the human body, it will die if it gets too cold. The same applies to business. What you need to know is, how cold is too cold for your business? It's called your breakeven. And here's the business principle: Always know your breakeven."

I wrote it down while Mike continued to talk.

Always know your breakeven.

"You need to answer this question: How much does it cost you to operate your business every week? How much rent, electricity, wages—everything. Got it?"

"Yeah."

"When you know that figure, you have your business temperature, if it gets below that, it's too cold and you won't survive."

"Makes sense."

"Now don't go about this like a scrooge. Just because you can survive at near-freezing doesn't mean you need to live in an igloo. When you're working out your weekly expenses, don't forgo the luxuries. You want this business to be a pleasure to work in, not a place for hobos."

"OK," I said, writing frantically to keep up.

"And another thing: you have machines that need servicing right?"

"Yeah."

"Same in my business. We have big, expensive trucks, like your printing machines. We have forklifts, cars and other machines. Your weekly expenses need to include maintenance costs. If anything breaks down, it costs you a fortune in lost production. You can't afford that. All our machines are serviced on time with the best parts; we never skimp on that. We renew our entire fleet regularly. That's why we have one of the best on-time delivery records in the industry. So, to reiterate what I've said: You're going for the ideal business here Jonnie and you need to know what that costs to run every week. Got it?"

"Yep. I'll start working on it straight away."

"Good. Oh, by the way, the best way to work this out is take an average of your last 3 or 4 months of expenses. That will give you a realistic figure."

"OK, thanks."

"Well that's all. Remember, get that Richard guy to start reporting daily."

"Yes, will do."

"Good. OK Jonnie gotta fly. Talk next week."

"Thanks Mike."

The business temperature was an interesting analogy. My guess was that it should have been a lot warmer around here, but right now, it was like the arctic and I was freezing my butt off. No wonder I was miserable. I hated the cold. It was time to find out and get the real numbers. I was going to need Sally's help with this.

I buzzed her. "Sally, can you get me a list of our expenses for the past 3 or 4 months?"

"You mean what we've paid or everything?" she asked.

I sighed. Depressing. "Everything. I need to work out our breakeven. It's an order from Mike."

"Right," she said. "I'll get onto it now."

"Thanks Sally." I sensed she knew whatever Mike wanted me to do was going to be good for us. But I felt that before it got better, it might get worse.

Now I needed to talk with Richard. I sent him a text.

"Hey Richard can you come by the office today? Got a few things I need to discuss."

"Can we talk on the phone? I want to make another sales call."

"No come to the office. I can wait until after your sales calls."

"OK I have a gap now so I'll head over."

"Thanks."

Richard arrived in his usual stylish suit, hair, gold watch and shiny shoes. I was at my desk working over the numbers Sally had given me when he popped his head in the door.

"Hey John, what's up?" he said jovially.

"Thanks for coming Richard. Take a seat." My stomach was doing somersaults but I kept hearing Mike's voice in my head. *"If he's making daily sales calls then he can damn well report his stats daily."* I really wasn't good at this management stuff. Maybe I wasn't cut out for the business owner role after all.

"So listen Richard, I know you said you work differently and all that, but I need you to report your stats daily, like everyone else." I had an annoying kind of nervous quiver in my voice. I hated doing this.

"Oh, you're not serious John?" he said.

I suddenly felt a little annoyed. "Look, you're making daily sales calls, so you can report them, like everyone else. I need to know what activity is going on each week so I can know if we're getting better or worse."

He didn't say anything, he just looked at me. There was a tense silence for a while. Then he said, "OK John, I get it. Fine. What do I report again?"

I was so relieved. I pulled out some paper and wrote them down: sales, number of quotes, number of appointments. I passed him the list.

He smiled. "OK, so I report these to Sally, right?"

"Yep, by 9am each day, whatever you did the day before."

"OK, was that all?" he asked.

"Yeah, and thanks Richard. I appreciate it."

"Hey, don't mention it." He lifted up his hand for a high-five.

"My man," I said, wanting to get back to our friendly banter. "Hey, what ya working on?"

"The Federal Printing Group looks like they'll be giving us a big order. I put in the tender today. It's tight, but worth it. We'll get our foot further in the door." That was one of his wholesale accounts he'd secured.

"How big?" I asked.

"Well, you will have to see it in the stats," he joked.

I laughed. Richard was my man.

"OK, I gotta go," he said.

We bumped fists and he left.

Back to my number grinding, but I felt great now that I had Richard fully onboard.

WEEK 4

I couldn't believe the numbers. It was costing a little over $9,000 per week to run this business. That means I had to make $9,000 per week in *profit* just to breakeven.

Of course, we weren't spending that because I was skimping on things and not paying certain bills because we didn't have the cash. But $9,000? That was insane. The revenue last year was just over $500,000. To make $9,000 a week, the revenue needed to be at least $30,000 a week. And that's with a healthy margin, not the tight margins of the wholesale orders.

I felt sick in my stomach looking at the numbers. My instinct was telling me I had to cut back. I had to save on costs somehow. But then I remembered Mike saying, *don't be a scrooge*. I looked up at Mandela's picture in my office and at the quote under it:

I never lose; I either win or learn.

Right now, I was losing a lot, which means I was learning a lot, but I didn't feel like it. It was time for some *Queen*. It was late and no one else was in the office, just me doing the usual late-night gig. Another large wholesale order with tiny margins required Betty to run all night and someone willing to work for little pay. Yeah, me, the "entrepreneur."

We Are the Champions started but I didn't sing along. I kept going over this one question: How the hell was I going to triple this business? I figured out I needed to be making $1.5 million in sales, with typical retail margin, to breakeven. There was no way Joe could sell that much.

Richard probably could, but he sold wholesale and those margins were dismal. He'd have to sell $10 million and that still probably wasn't enough.

It was a conundrum. The only thing that kept me from flipping out, throwing the wrench and swearing fluffy-duck all over the place, was Mike. I had a call with him tomorrow, in just over 8 hours. I was sure he'd have a solution. I started to hum along near the end of the fourth verse.

I am not going to lose.

I am a champion.

I am going to win.

"Mike!" I said, like a kid who dropped his ice cream.

"Jonnie, what's up pal? You sound like you just got out of bed."

"Haven't been to bed yet."

"Oh, I see. Tough week?"

"Nine thousand, Mike. I need to be making nine thousand a week or I'll freeze to death. That means I need to triple this business or I'm screwed."

"Yeah, thought so. No surprise," he said.

"What? You mean you knew it was this bad?"

"Yeah, a lot of businesses struggle because they are operating below their freezing level, below their breakeven. It's masked by things like credit cards, overdrafts, loans, delayed payment of bills and taxes. But the truth is, a lot of them are standing in the Arctic, in a swimsuit, freezing their asses off."

"What am I going to do, Mike? I have to cut costs."

"Well, first, let me ask you a question. Did you include any pay for yourself in the nine thousand per week?"

"Yeah."

"How much?"

"Five hundred dollars."

"I'm guessing that makes you the most underpaid employee of the business."

"Yeah."

"Let me guess, you figured you can make up the difference from the profits, but the only problem is, you have none."

"Yeah." He wasn't making me feel any better.

"So really, if you paid yourself even a basic salary, then you need to make ten thousand."

"Are you trying to make me feel worse?"

He laughed. "No, Jonnie. Here's the thing: all I am doing is getting you to see what is really in front of you. Any misery or upset you feel is not because of me; it's because you are finally seeing your business as it is. I know it's tough, but it's the first step to improving anything. Before you set out on a journey, you need to know where you are and where you are going. Believe it or not," he continued, "it's a giant step forward."

"I enjoyed being ignorant. It was easier."

"Yeah right, ignorance is bliss. What a load of rubbish. That's for the losers and you aren't a loser."

"So, how do I fix it Mike?"

"Simple. Business is like baking a cake."

"I thought it was a thermometer?"

"That was last week."

"It's hard to keep up with you."

"That's what everybody says," he chimed. "Now, how do you make the perfect cake?"

"Ask my wife to make it?"

"Ha, ha, very funny. No, you follow the perfect recipe," he said. "It's the combination of the different ingredients, all mixed together, that make the perfect cake. The cake we want to make in business is the cake of *profit*. You already have your list of ingredients—each step of the stairway to profit is an ingredient. Now, how much promotion do you need? How many leads do you need? How many appointments and so on. What you need to do is work out how much is needed, on average, to bake the perfect cake."

I was scribbling madly.

"And here's the thing. Once you've got the perfect ingredients, how do you make a bigger cake?" he asked.

"Er ... use more ingredients?" I guessed.

"Exactly. You see, ingredients are the key. With them, you can improve the cake. Same with your profit. To improve the profit, focus on improving the ingredients. So, here's the business principle: Always focus on what you can improve."

I wrote it in my journal.

Always focus on what you can improve.

He continued, "Once you know how many leads are needed to make the sales you need, you then focus on the promotion to generate the necessary leads. That's what you put your attention on, because that's what you can improve. Make sense?"

"Yes, but what about profit margin? No point selling jobs at cost, right?"

"Great question and I was going to ask you about that. But first, did you have a chat with Richard?"

"Yes, he's onboard now and reporting daily."

"Good. What are his stats like?" Mike asked.

"Not much activity. He's mostly doing appointments, working on deals."

"Right, how does that compare to Joe?"

"Err, let me check." I had MetaPulse open on my computer and I pulled up both of their stats.

Here's what they looked like for the past 2 weeks:

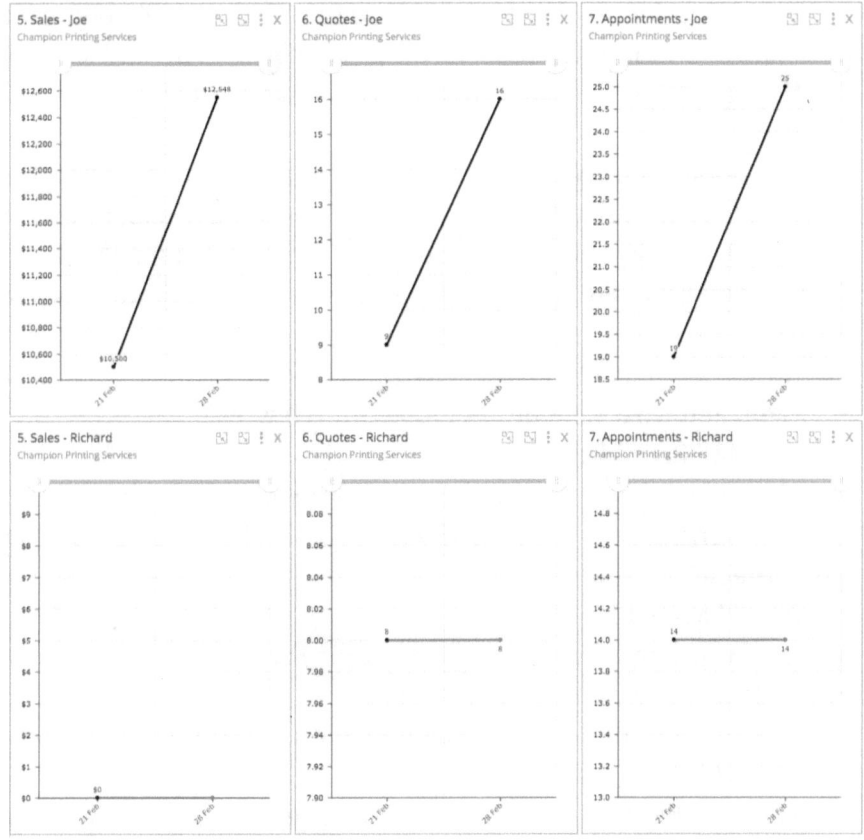

Joe's was up over the last few weeks with over 25 appointments per week; Richard had 14 per week. I shared the data with Mike.

"So, Joe is doing almost twice the number of appointments as Richard?" Mike asked.

"Yeah, well, you know Richard has to spend more time with the clients because they are bigger orders. They take longer to work out. Plus, he's building a relationship with them," I said, in Richard's defense.

"Is that what Richard told you?"

"Well, yeah."

"OK Jonnie, here's what I need you to do. Work out the total sales for the past 12 months; break it down in sales by Richard and sales by Joe. Then work out the total profit of each. Make sense?"

"Yep."

"OK, good. Now, you may be wondering how to calculate the ingredients factor I mentioned earlier. Like, how many appointments does it take to make a sale; you should be able to get that number from the stats you have. For example, Joe did what—25 appointments last week?"

"Yeah."

"Right, and what were his total sales for the week?"

"$12,548," I replied.

"OK, so you know for Joe, 25 appointments equals about $12k, so that's ... hang on ... 12k divided by 25 ... that about $500 per appointment."

"Yeah," I agreed.

"So, if you wanted Joe to make $15k for the week, then you need him to do 30 appointments. Make sense?"

I divided $15k by $500 and came up with 30, so yeah, that made sense. "I get it."

"Now, another way to go about this is to get Joe to get his average sale per appointment up to $600. That's another ingredient you could play with. You could also keep that as another stat."

"Cool. I like this."

"And do the same with Richard," he said.

"OK, great. Thanks Mike."

"The key is to set the quota and to tell your team what you expect, each week."

"OK, set weekly quotas, understood," I said.

"Now, to answer your question about profit margin, you need to have a fixed policy regarding pricing. You need a standard markup. Discounting, pricing a job lower than your standard markup, needs to be approved by you. Personally, I believe discounting is a way to avoid the effort of selling. The approach we use when we provide a quote is to itemise what the client is buying, as well as all the key benefits and features. If the client asks for a discount, we ask them what item, feature or benefit they want to remove, to reduce the price."

I was writing frantically to keep up.

"You've mentioned you have an on-time delivery guarantee or it's free," he said.

"Yes," I replied.

"And you offer this for every job?"

"Yes."

"Well, that's an added benefit. If a client asks for a discount, they lose that benefit."

"I like that," I said.

"Same applies to the quality of paper; if they want a cheaper price, offer to reduce the quality. You see, what I find is client's don't like to remove things and you're assigning value to things they usually aren't. This approach tends to reduce discounting and it keeps the jobs profitable. It also provides the client with a way to truly compare your products and services against the competition."

"You're a genius. Thanks, Mike."

"Pleasure. OK, talk next week."

"Yep."

So, Joe's average was $500 per appointment. I wondered what Richard's was. But before I did that, I needed Sally to give me those sales numbers.

I buzzed her, "Hey, Sally?"

"Yes?"

"Can you work out the total sales for Richard and Joe for the past 12 months? And also get me the invoices for each job. I need to work out what the profit margin is on them."

"Another project from Mike?" she asked.

"How'd you guess?"

"It's Tuesday," she said. "Everything changes on a Tuesday."

"You're right."

"OK, I'll get on it, as soon as I'm finished with these deliveries. I want to get them out today so my stats are up this week."

"No argument from me. Thanks, Sally."

Before I tell Richard and Joe about our new pricing policy, and the "removing the benefit" method Mike mentioned, I probably needed to work out what the best markup should be first! One thing for certain, no more on-time guarantees for those damn wholesale jobs.

WEEK 5

Numbers. That's all I seemed to be looking at these days. After a week of late-night printing, here I was, in the office, on a Sunday, going over all of the sales for the past 12 months. I looked over at my shrine of *Queen* hanging on the wall. I had a photo of Freddie, standing with his hand in the air, in front of a massive crowd at Wembley Stadium. Live Aid concert 1985. Same year Mike introduced me to the band.

"A pleasure cruise this is not, right Fred?" I said to him.

He didn't reply.

After 12 hours of number crunching, what I discovered shocked me. Joe's jobs were pretty standard and his pricing markup worked out to roughly about 60% profit. Sometimes more, sometimes less, but generally in that range. Overall, he'd sold $452,000 worth of printing in the past twelve months, for an average of just over $9,400 per week. The gross profit he generated for the business was $271,000, less his salary of $65,000 and other expenses—call it $80k all up—he was making me $191k per year. I was surprised.

Richard, on the other hand, had sold less! That surprised me even more. Just under $300,000. But the profit on his jobs took longer to work out. I had to go through every invoice, looking at the paper type and quantities so I could roughly work out the cost of the job and, of course, the profit. Even being conservative with my costs, Richard had generated a total of about $30k profit. Less his $100k salary and perks, I was out of pocket about $80,000 over the last year. That's where my salary and profits were going.

I was utterly depressed. This had to change. Richard's wholesale strategy was killing my business. Hell, it was killing me because I was the one doing the work every night for these big jobs. The idea that we'd squeeze extra profits out of bulk orders of raw materials didn't stack up either, because it became evident that every job required something a little different.

Added to this was the dismal fact that Richard's average appointment-to-sale ratio was less than Joe's; it was $446, yet he was doing less than a third of Joe's appointments.

Lo and behold, Joe was my star salesman. Quiet, unassuming, dress-the-same-every-day Joe was generating nearly ten times the profit of the slick, well-dressed, outgoing Richard. I would never have believed it.

I really didn't want to sack Richard. I considered him an asset. We simply had to figure out a different strategy because this obviously wasn't working. But before taking any drastic action, I was going to wait until my Tuesday talk with Mike. I was sure he'd point me in the right direction.

"Mike, I got the sales numbers!" I said like a kid whose ice cream had melted.

"Let's hear it."

"Joe's making over me almost $200k a year, but Richard's costing me more than $80k."

"And I bet you thought it was the other way around?"

"Yeah, well I knew the wholesale jobs were tight, but I guess I underestimated the value Joe was creating."

"It's a common mistake and from what you've told me, Joe keeps to himself and gets the job done."

"Yeah."

"Whereas Richard is always telling you about some great deal."

"Yeah, but hang on, I didn't tell you Richard does that."

"True, call it an educated guess. Here's another one, I bet Richard bags Joe behind his back. Little snide comments here and there, am I right?"

I had to think for a moment. "A little … maybe," I said.

"You'll notice it more now that I've pointed it out. Listen, Jonnie, this is going to be tough, but I need you to trust me on this."

I noticed the sudden change in his tone. It was more serious. "What's going to be tough?"

"I think Richard has been taking you for a ride, based on the stats and what you've told me. I know his type. I've had to deal with plenty of them. But we have to be smart about this. You said he works with mostly wholesale clients?"

"Yeah."

"Right, I want you to send me the client details of all the sales he has made."

"Why? What are you going to do?"

"Like I said, I need you to trust me on this. Don't worry about it for now. I'm going to do some investigation. Let's just keep this to ourselves."

"But Mike, I can't keep letting him sell these wholesale jobs; they're killing me financially, they're keeping me below freezing and they're busting my business thermometer."

"I know, I know, but like I said, if I'm right about this guy, it could get a lot worse. Remember the vampires, the champion killers?"

"You think Richard is one?"

"Like I said, could be or maybe he's just a loser who has gotten away with slacking off because up until now, you've been too soft on him. But anyway, let's get down to the important stuff. Did you work out your ingredients?"

I still had questions about Richard, but I let them go. I had to trust Mike. "Yeah, I went over Joe's numbers with him and instantly, the next day, he upped his average sale per appointment to $550."

"Great, I like Joe."

"Yeah, he was real proud, came and showed me the orders, which come to think of it, he's rarely ever done."

"He's a champion. And what about appointments? Did he do more?"

"He did. He's going for 40 per week. We worked out that if he does 40 appointments at an average of $500, he'll do almost a $1 million in sales a year."

"Beautiful."

"Yeah, it's incredible. He's really pumped. I've never seen him so enthusiastic."

"That's the power of these principles, Jonnie. Business becomes more fun when you can see the results."

"True. Oh, by the way, he asked me about bonuses. This has always been a touchy subject, because well, I can never afford it. Got any advice?"

"Yeah, but we'll cover that next week or so. Tell him you'll work it out."

"OK, will do. So, what's the lesson for this week?"

"Business is like a light switch."

"Not a cake?"

"No, a light switch. If you want the light to turn on, what do you do?"

"Flick the light switch," I said.

"That's right. Every time you flick the switch, *bam*—the light goes on. It works, every time."

"Unless the bulb is broken."

"Correct or there could be a fault in the wire or the electricity could be cut off. But all things being equal, if you want light, flick the switch. Simple, right?"

"Yeah, but I'm waiting for the punchline."

"I know, but you see, this is too simple. And the simple things get missed all the time. That's why I'm driving this home. If you want light, flick the switch. If you want sales, you need to promote. Promotion is the first step on the stairway to profit. But promotion is something people over-complicate. They try to come up with gimmicks, new slogans and fancy offers. Millions get wasted on promotion. But all they have to do is flick the switch. Here's the principle: What worked before will work again."

I wrote it down on a new page in my book.

What worked before will work again.

"I want you to get all your monthly sales for the past 5 years; plot them on a graph, using MetaPulse. Look for your highest-ever months of sales. Then figure out what promotion you were doing then."

"That's it?" I asked.

"Yes, because whatever it was, it will work again. Don't guess; get the stats and ask your team what promotion was being done during the two months prior to those sales. Got it?"

"Yeah, why the two months?"

"Because it can take up to eight weeks to see the effect of a successful campaign."

"Oh, I didn't know that."

"Most people don't, because they don't track their stats, so they miss the correlation. But when you figure what worked, we're going to flick the switch on that campaign again."

"OK, great! I'll get on it."

"Alright, talk next week."

"Er … Mike, I still have my attention on Richard. What do you want me to do?"

"Send me the client details of the sales he's made. That's all. For now, keep focusing on your business and put your attention on your champions. I'll let you know next week what we'll do with Richard."

"OK, thanks, Mike."

"Pleasure."

I felt uneasy about the Richard situation. Mike seemed so serious, but this promotion idea was something to focus on.

I buzzed Sally. "Hey, Sally!"

"What is it this week?" she said. "You want to know how many pieces of paper I picked off the floor for the past 12 months?"

"Close," I said.

"What?" she said in a motherly tone of voice.

"Monthly sales for the past five years."

"Does Mike think we're the Bureau of Economic Analysis?"

"Maybe."

"Fine, when do you want it, because I'm not going to let my stats go down. I hate that red line on that graph, MetaPulse always colors the line red when it's down. It's evil. It clashes with my pink blouse."

"I was thinking the same thing," I said. "Listen, this project has to do with booming our sales and once you have the stats together, I'll most likely need your help and Joe's help working out the next step. So, how about we go for getting it done by Friday afternoon and we meet in my office?"

"Coffee and cake?"

"Of course."

"OK, deal. But I'm only doing it for the coffee and cake."

"Of course."

She clicked off. She was a champion, no doubt about it.

I think I managed to get about fifteen hours sleep between Tuesday and Friday. Maybe I needed to start keeping a stat on that and graph it in MetaPulse? Mike did say that if you wanted to improve something, you needed to measure it first. But then I yawned; it was tiring just thinking about it. Coffee—that was the solution.

As I got up to leave my office for the kitchen, Sally came in with a big cake.

"Wow, that looks nice. Chocolate is my favorite. I'm going to get the coffee."

"I just filled the pot," she said.

"Great."

As I crossed the noisy factory floor, I walked into Joe, who was smiling at me. "Hey, Joe," I yelled over the thumping sounds of Betty.

"John, I averaged $600 today!" he said proudly.

"Awesome work." I patted him on the back. "That's brilliant." He was beaming back at me and I realized this was how I normally treated Richard. There was a brief uncomfortable silence between us. "Hey, I'm getting the coffee. Sally's in my office with the cake; you better be quick or there will be none left."

He smiled, nodded and headed off. As I watched him go, I felt a sudden wave of admiration for the guy. Day in, day out, he traveled the road, come rain, hail or shine, meeting new people to sell them stuff for me. He'd never complained. Never taken a sick day and loyally wore the white shirt with my logo on it. I couldn't believe I hadn't seen it before: he was a champion. I wanted to chase after him and give him a hug, but it would have probably creeped him out. Instead, I turned and did my job as the assigned coffee boy, happy to be waiting on my champions.

After too much cake and not enough coffee, we'd isolated the top sales months. Figuring out the actual promotional campaign we were running at the time was a bit more difficult. I remember spending money on all sorts of things, like radio ads, mailings and Google ads.

But, nothing really corresponded to the 2-month window Mike had stipulated. The problem was, the highest months on record were almost 4 years ago. I could hardly remember last week, let alone 4 years.

Until Joe, lost in thought, remembered something. "Didn't you hire that marketing consultant around that time?" he asked me.

"Oh yeah, that guy, Mr. Guarantee or it's free?"

"Yeah, wasn't that when you changed to online marketing?" Joe asked.

"Yeah."

"Before that, we used to send out that old flyer with the $100 voucher," he said. "That's what the prior owners always did."

"Yes, of course," said Sally. "I remember that."

I only vaguely remembered and my ignorance must have been obvious because Sally looked at me and said to Joe, "He can't remember. There must be a copy of one around here somewhere."

"I'll ask Drew; he'll know," Joe said and off he went.

The couch in my office was feeling rather comfortable and I could feel myself getting drowsy.

"John, you're falling asleep. Here, have some more coffee. No more cake for you," said mother Sally.

I shook my head and slapped my face. A few minutes later, Joe came back with a box.

"Here they are." He handed one to Sally and one to me.

I remember them now, bright orange writing, a fake looking $100 note, with a headline that said "$100 off your next order." These had my logo on it, so we'd obviously copied the old format.

"We used to mail these out every week," said Sally.

"And I used to drop them in letter boxes while on the road," said Joe.

Mike's voice echoed in my head: *What worked before will work again.*

"This will work again," I said, feeling more awake. "Whatever we were doing before, we'll do it again."

"Why'd we stop?" asked Sally.

"That marketing guru told me it was old-school and we needed to go digital," I recalled. Sally had the revengeful look of a mother whose child had just been bullied. If that marketing guru ever showed up again, I don't think he'd leave this place in one piece.

With Mike's weekly mission accomplished, Sally distributed the rest of the cake to Drew and the other factory crew. She returned to my office and told me to go home. Tiffany had dinner on the table and I was not allowed to be late.

Exhausted, I complied.

WEEK 6

While waiting for Mike's call, I was looking over the stats of the prior week. This is what they looked like:

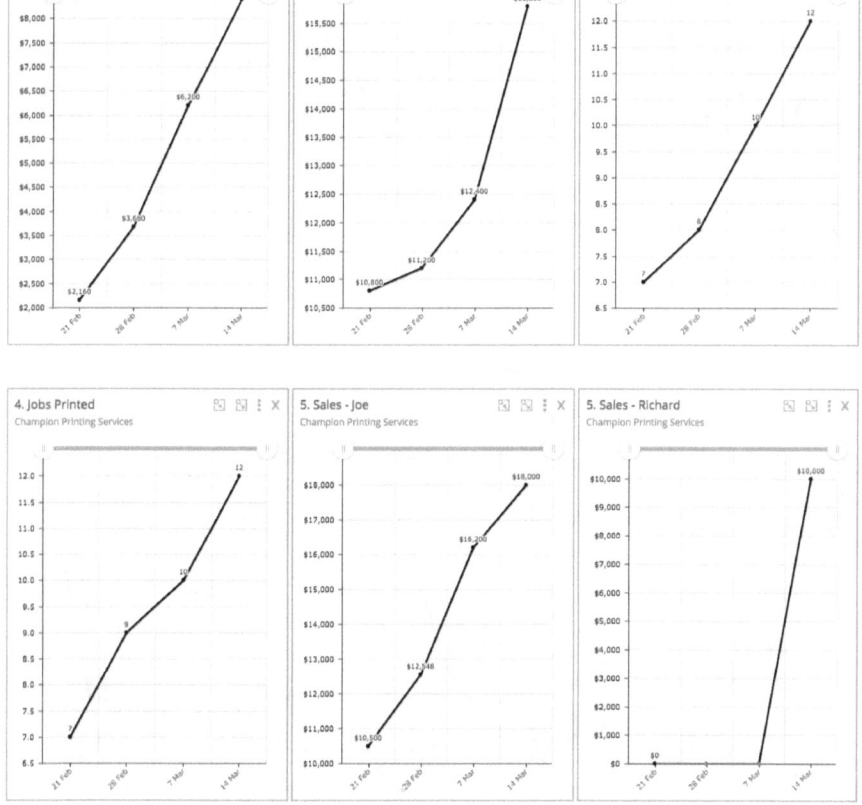

TONY MELVIN

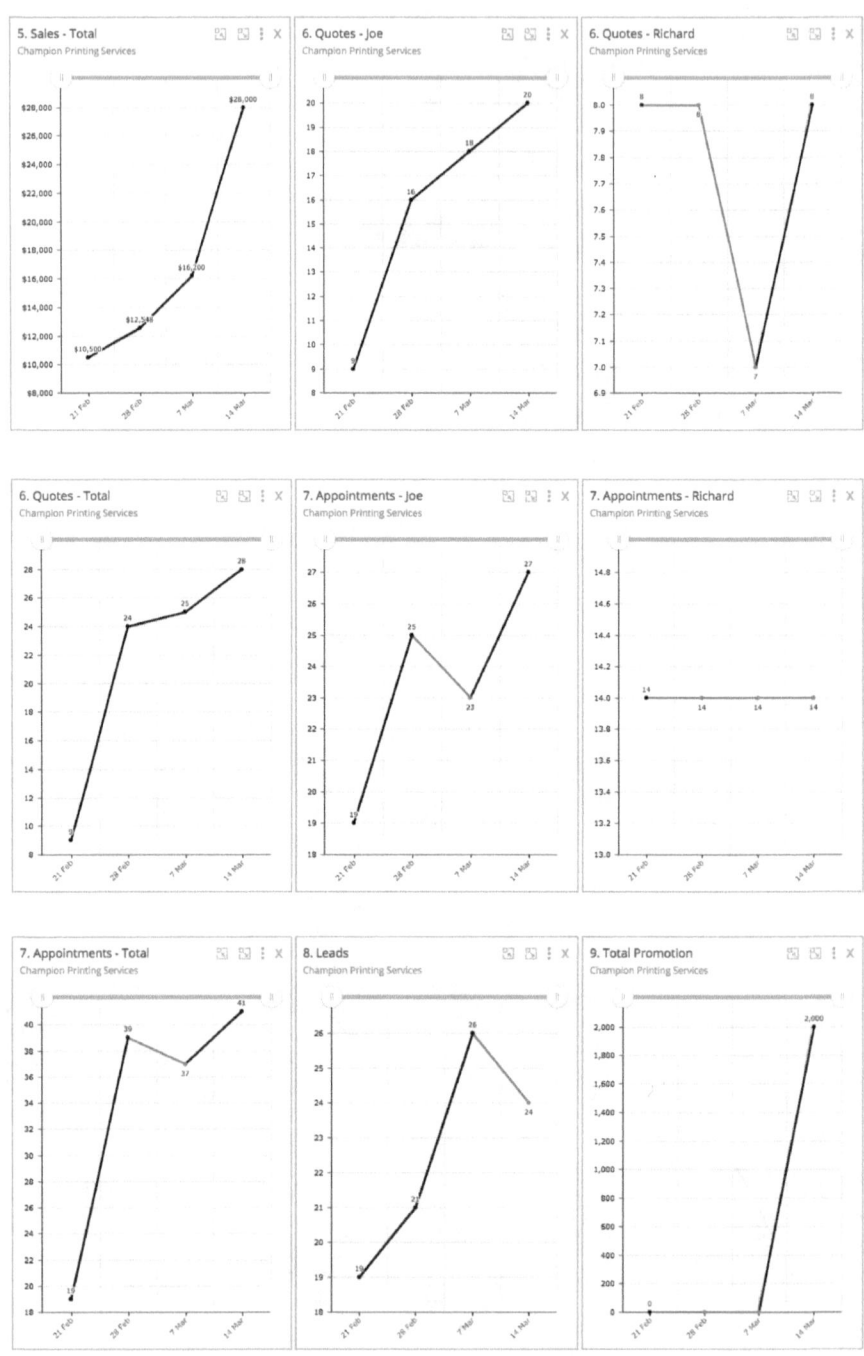

Things were picking up, mostly thanks to Joe who did a whopping $18k in sales last week, with an average profit margin of 65%, following our new pricing policy. Drew was also mindful of deliveries and didn't want his stats going down either. In fact, last week, I had to wait until 6pm before Betty-the-printer was free. Although he normally finished around 4pm, he said he had to get this job done so it could be delivered this week. He said he and Sally had worked it out. Although I was glad he was dedicated, I was a bit worried he'd be wanting overtime pay. I asked Sally about it.

She said, "Don't be silly. He knows there's no overtime pay. But he also knows that we need to get these deliveries done so we get our normal pay."

"And he didn't mind?"

"Not at all; he's part of the team, John. He knows the deal."

He was a champion.

So overall, things were looking good. Richard was still reporting the same number of appointments and only one sale. He had been in the office briefly the day before. He gave me the usual high-five, but I had to fake enthusiasm. He had to prod me to ask him, "What ya working on?" That's when I noticed it, just like Mike said I would. "Got some big deals, not small startup packages like Joe." The snide comment. I really had to bite my tongue, because what I wanted to say was, "Joe has sold nearly six times more than you in the past four weeks." But I smiled, told him I was busy and walked off.

I was dreading what Mike had to say. It was the first time I'd felt apprehension about our weekly call.

At 8 a.m. my phone buzzed. "Chairman of the Bureau of Economic Analysis for you," said Sally.

I laughed. "Very funny; put him through." But she already had.

"What's funny?" said Mike.

"Oh, Mike ... Sally was just making a joke. She thinks you really work for the Bureau of Economic Analysis."

He laughed. "Well after today's phone call, she'll probably think I work for the Justice Department."

"Really, why?"

"No easy way to say this Jonnie, but ol' Richard is a dick and he's been screwing you big time."

"What? How?"

"Jonnie, before I share this information with you, I need you to keep your cool and do exactly as I say."

Despite my blood boiling in anger, my stomach did a flip. "What the hell is going on, Mike?"

"Richard is a vampire. I know his end game and we need to be very careful how we tackle this. I've been down this road before, Jonnie. So, I need you to do exactly what I say."

I breathed. "OK, what?"

"I've got a lawyer friend of mine coming to your office tomorrow morning. His name is Jack. He'll be there at 8 a.m. I want you to make sure Richard arrives later, at 8.30. Jack will handle everything; just follow his lead."

"Mike, what's this guy cost? I can't afford a lawyer."

"Jonnie, this one is on me. Don't worry about the cost."

"Mike, I can't ask you to do that."

"You didn't. You are my friend. I help my friends."

"But Mike, to send a lawyer down here must be costing you a fortune."

"Not really. Jack is doing it as a favor. I pay his firm about a million bucks a year and besides, we've been good buddies for a long time."

"Wow! A million bucks? He's probably coming in his own Learjet."

"Nah, he's coming in my Gulfstream."

"Really? I was joking. You've got a plane?"

"G600 model, just upgraded."

"Cool. Can I borrow it some time?"

"Sure, just say the word."

"I was joking. Again."

"Well, I wasn't. Anyway, enough about Richard. How's your week been?"

I filled him in on the progress: Joe's stellar results, Drew and Sally's collaboration to get deliveries up and the coffee and cake meeting.

"Wonderful, got a real team of champions there."

"Yeah, but we've still got a long way to go to get above nine thousand a week."

"Well, I think after tomorrow, that won't be a problem," he said.

"Really?" I couldn't imagine what a lawyer could do to change the business around in a single day, unless he gave me a cut of his million in fees.

"Yeah," Mike said.

"So, what's the lesson for this week?" I asked.

"We've kind of already covered it. You see, business is like a garden."

"We've ditched the light switch?"

"Yeah, it's a garden now."

"You know, cake was my favorite. I like cake."

"Well, if you don't tend to it like a garden, you'll never have time to eat the cake."

"Now you're being cryptic. How so?"

"Because you'll be dead," he said harshly.

"Now you've totally lost me. And creeped me out," I said.

"You've got to get rid of the weeds fast. Let the flowers bloom."

"You know, I run a printing business, not a plant nursery."

"Richard is a weed. If you don't get rid of him quick he'll kill off the rest of the flowers you cherish. Including you."

"You're still creeping me out. Can't we talk about cake?"

"After tomorrow, yes."

"So, that's it. Business is a garden, so get rid of the weeds fast?"

"Yes. Poetic, don't you think?" he asked.

"Normally, you give me an analogy and then a sensible written principle that applies. But this is just an analogy. It's still kind of cryptic, like a fortune cookie."

"Alright. Your business has no place for losers or champion killers. Kill them off quickly before they kill you. How's that?"

"Direct. I'm writing it in my book."

> Your business has no place for losers or champion killers.
> Kill them off quickly before they kill you.

I asked, "Are you making this up as you go along?"

"A little."

"If you didn't have a multimillion dollar business and a Gulfstream jet, I'd be worried."

"You see, stats prove everything."

"True. Hey, Mike?"

"Yeah?"

"Thanks, buddy."

"You bet. Good luck tomorrow. Call me when you've finished the meeting with Jack. And, Jonnie ..."

"What?"

"Trust Jack; he's the best. Just follow his lead."

"I will."

"See ya."

I sat in my office, in silence for a long time. I had a lawyer on his way, flying in a fancy Gulfstream to meet with me and my employee. I still had no idea what Richard had done. Glancing down at my notebook, I figured he was about to be killed off quickly, according to this last business principle. But I decided not to ponder it anymore. Mike was backing me up and making sure it would come out alright. He truly was my best friend.

I was both eager and apprehensive about tomorrow. Still, I needed to make sure Richard was there. I sent him a text.

> "Hey Richard. Need you in the office tomorrow at 8.30a. Got a meeting with a guy. It's a big deal. Need you here with me."

I figured appealing to his deal-hungry nature would ensure he'd turn up. Of course, it wasn't the kind of deal he was thinking of. But it was a big deal, to me anyway. And to Mike.

"Sure. Who's the client?"

"It's a surprise," I replied.

"Lol - OK, see you 2moro."

I was in the office early. I figured it needed a clean. An expensive lawyer coming to visit brought on a nervous reaction similar to meeting the in-laws for the first time. I desperately wanted to impress, but truthfully, I was afraid of retribution, of any kind. Everything from dust to coffee type was potential grounds for disapproval or punishment. So, I not only cleaned my office from top to bottom, I also bought every type of coffee and milk known to man.

I finally sat at my desk, sipping my morning cuppa, when at precisely 8 a.m., the phone buzzed. "John, Jack is here to see you."

As pre-arranged with Sally, I said, "Thank you, Sally, I'll be there in a moment."

Sally had no idea why Jack was there. She was a bit surprised yesterday when, after my call with Mike, I didn't call her and ask for our sales records dating back to the eighteenth century. I told her about the meeting with Jack, a friend of Mike's and that Richard was due to join us at 8.30.

When I reached the reception area, Jack was chatting with Sally. He was tall, impeccably dressed, with black, slightly graying hair. He had that commanding air of someone who was smart, athletic, well-educated, good-looking and…*really* rich. When I shook his hand, he had a firm handshake and looked me right in the eye. "Great to meet you, Jonnie."

"Pleasure to meet you too. Thanks for coming all this way," I said.

"Don't mention it. I have to do what Mike tells me; he's my client," he laughed.

I laughed too. Bit too loud. So did Sally and I swear she was blushing.

I regained my composure. "Shall we?" I gestured to my office.

"Yes, pleasure to meet you, Sally," he said as he shook her hand.

"You too, Jack." Her face now matched her pink blouse.

I waited until I got Jack in the office and shut the door, so we could talk without having to yell above the din of the machinery. "Can I get you coffee?"

"No, that's fine Jonnie. Let's go cover what's about to happen so we're prepared."

"OK."

"What did Mike tell you?"

"Not much, to be honest. He just said to follow your lead, let you run the meeting."

"Right, are you OK with that?" he asked.

"Sure, although I'd like to know what Richard's been up to," I said as I took a sip of coffee.

"He's been ripping you off. His wholesale clients—he owns those companies. They are shells. No employees. He sells the job at retail, screws you down on price and makes a killing in between, while at the same time, he is taking a salary from you."

I was flabbergasted. I dropped my cup.

"I know it's a shock. His game plan, no doubt, is to drive you close to bankruptcy and then buy the business off you for a steal. Of course, he'll make it look like he's doing you a favor, to 'save' you."

I couldn't believe it. But why? Why do that? I hadn't done anything to him. I had trusted him.

Jack no doubt could see the turmoil I was under.

"Jonnie." He said it loud to get my attention.

"Yeah?"

"Some people think the only way to get ahead in life is by stepping on others. To steal, cheat and manipulate. Richard is one of those people. But don't worry, you're in good hands. Today, it ends."

I saw him glance up at the Mandela picture behind my desk, with the quote about losing, winning and learning. He smiled. "Richard's about to learn a very valuable lesson and you're about to win."

I feigned a smile. I wondered, how much had this scumbag made off me over the last 14 months?

Jack and I chatted a little while I cleaned my coffee mess off the floor. He was probably trying to take my mind off the bad news. He noticed the *Queen* memorabilia around my office.

"Queen fan, hey?"

"Yeah."

"Mike loves them as well."

"He introduced me, back in the sixth grade," I said. "We used to play, sing and head-bang to them in his bedroom. We even dressed up like them once, for a fancy dress party."

Jack laughed. "Now *that* I'd like to see."

Jack looked out of my office and saw Richard coming across the factory floor. Despite being a scumbag, he was punctual—a punctual scumbag.

"Show time!" Jack said. "Just introduce me and I'll take it from there."

Richard opened the office door. "Good morning!" he said jovially.

Jovial scumbag. Suddenly, his fancy suit, slick hair and gold watch made me want to puke. I paid for those damn things with my sleepless nights and weekends. Time away from my wife and kids.

"Richard, this is Jack," I said with a despicable slur. It was the friendliest voice I could muster. He didn't seem to notice. All eyes were on Jack.

Jack stood and held out his hand. "Richard."

Richard shook Jack's hand and smiled. Smiling scumbag.

I saw Richard do a quick appraisal of Jack, taking in the suit, the style. He saw money. His first comment said it all.

"So, John says you've got a big deal for us?" Richard smiled while unbuttoning his fancy suit and taking a seat.

"Indeed," Jack said, going along.

"No wonder Joe's not here," Richard said, with a wink at me and a smirk that I wanted to wipe off his face with my coffee mug. Fluffy-duck scumbag.

Jack began with a clever line that immediately killed Richard's smirk. "Richard thanks for coming. Can I call you Dick?"

"Er… no, I prefer Richard."

"OK," Jack said. "I've got a deal I want to propose to you both. But first, I need to ask, do you mind if I record this meeting? Company policy, you see. Of course, it's not for my protection; it's more for you and if I may, more for the company." He smiled. "Because a deal such as this, if I promise something that is out of the ordinary, then it comes back on me. You, of course, won't be affected, but I will. So, hang on a second …" He pulled out a fancy little dictaphone and hit record. "Good, so any objections to recording this meeting?"

He looked at Richard, the scumbag.

"No, fine with me," the scumbag said.

"Jonnie?"

"Yeah, fine with me."

"OK, great! The first thing I want to discuss, in this deal, is ownership."

He leaned over and pulled out a thick folder from his briefcase. It was full of paperwork, methodically tabbed in sections. He plopped it on the table with a thud and pulled out a yellow legal pad. I looked over at Richard who returned my glance with a raised eyebrow, as if to say, "What the heck is this guy up to?"

"Right, here it is," Jack said. "So, first question: Richard, who owns these following companies?" He rattled off the six wholesale clients Richard had been making sales to all year.

I saw the color drain from Richard's face. He squirmed in his seat, frowned and cleared his throat. *Got ya.*

"I'm not sure what you mean," he mumbled.

"Oh, let me rephrase it," Jack said. "You own these companies, don't you Dick, except the last one, which is in your wife's name?"

Richard the dick was silent for a long time. I could feel my heart beating against my chest.

"I'm not sure what you're talking about, but even so, what difference does that make?" he said, cocky as hell.

"It makes all the difference," Jack replied. "Let me share something with you." He turned in his chair to face Richard. "What I'm about to tell you will trigger a fight-or-flight mechanism. You'll either want to run or you'll want to punch me in the face. But if you do either, by the end of the day, I will have a warrant to search your house and car. I will have a caveat put on every asset you own, including that Rolex watch. We'll issue a press release to the local media of your illegal conduct while under Jonnie's employment."

Geez, I was beginning to break out in a sweat just listening to Jack. I couldn't imagine what was going through Richard's mind.

"All I want to achieve in this meeting," Jack continued, "is what us lawyers call an 'out of court settlement'. It's faster, less painful and keeps the media out of it. Do you understand me, Dick?"

Richard was starting to fume; he shuffled in his chair again. "I asked you to call me Richard."

"Yes, but you've been screwing poor Jonnie here for over a year, so I think the name Dick is appropriate. Besides, it's quicker to say than Richard and I'm here as a favor for a friend and not charging my usual hours. You know, being a lawyer and all, I'm time-sensitive."

I couldn't help but smile. I loved Jack. He was my favorite lawyer in the world.

"Now, one more thing," Jack said. "I know you are probably thinking you should lawyer up. Let me tell you why that's a bad idea. If you go to a lawyer, he or she will take one look at that suit you're wearing—Armani, if I'm not mistaken. Nice cut—your Rolex, your Louis Vuitton shoes and they'll not only smell money, they'll see it. After a brief investigation into my firm and Jonnie's humble little business, said lawyer will conclude that he could easily bankrupt my client before it got anywhere near a court, so you'd have an easy case on your hands. They'd recommend a monthly retainer of about $10k to $20k and estimate a 6-month battle."

He paused while Richard looked away. When he turned back, Jack continued, "But here's something your lawyer won't know. Although I'm representing Jonnie here, my client is Mike. Mike pays me over a million dollars a year to handle his legal battles. I have 150 lawyers who work for me, forty dedicated to corporate law. After we presented Mike with our research on your colorful activities of the past year, you know what he said to me?"

Jack paused while Richard looked away again, shuffled in his seat and then looked back at Jack. "He said, cut a deal with him or bury him."

"Now, you may think that you haven't done anything illegal and a lawyer, to get your business, will tell you, we've got nothing concrete to go on. But, let me ask you a question: do you know what racketeering is?"

Richard shook his head.

"Racketeering is dishonest and fraudulent business dealings. Surprisingly, our justice system is so twisted that racketeering charges often exceed rape and other violent crimes. And although racketeering is non-violent, they put the convicted in the same jail as the murderers, armed robbers and gang members. Personally, I find it appalling. But that's the way our system works. So, here's the upshot, Dick. You make a deal today, right now or I'm going to throw everything at you, bankrupt you and make sure you serve time in jail. And I'll spread it all over the media, just for kicks."

Holy fluffy-duck. Jack was ruthless. I almost felt sorry for Richard. Almost.

After a long pause, with Jack staring intently, Richard finally spoke. In a meek, flat voice, he asked, "What kind of deal are you talking about?'

"I've got the terms drawn up here." He pulled an official-looking document out of his big folder. "You are welcome to read it, but let me give it to you in layman's terms. Firstly, you pay Jonnie damages of $118,000 immediately." Richard shuffled in his chair and coughed.

Jack continued, "That's basically the wages he paid you because he thought you were working for him, but you weren't. Secondly, you assign all your retail clients over to Jonnie, including records of the sale transactions and inform all clients that you were bought out by Champion Printing. Third, you agree to a non-compete clause in the city and surrounding area for 5 years. If you agree to those terms, we will not press charges and the matter will remain confidential. You'll be free to continue your life."

Richard looked at Jack, but he avoided me. I realized since Jack began his onslaught, Richard hadn't looked me in the eye once.

"I don't have $118,000," he said meekly.

"Yes, you do. On your Black AMEX. Jonnie can run it now, plus the 4% charge, of course. They'll probably call for such a large transaction; you wait here until they do and confirm the amount. Then, you sign the documents and you're off."

I wondered how he knew Richard had a Black AMEX. Richard shook his head. He was hunched over, sweating and breathing heavily.

"I want to read this document first," Richard said.

"Good idea," Jack replied. "Jonnie, I'll take that cup of coffee now, black, no sugar."

"Right." I got up and left the office.

God, that was intense. But what a deal. If Richard agreed, I'd have $118k in the bank, which would eliminate my overdraft and I'd get a bunch of new retail clients. I wondered how much money Richard had made. He sold about $300,000 worth; if he did an average markup, he'd have made about $150k. That was rightfully mine too, but I was guessing Jack was going for a quick settlement, so it was done. That's what I wanted too.

When I got back to the office, Richard appeared to have given up reading the document. He said, "Where do I sign?"

Jack, ever so helpful, said, "Initial every page and sign the last one. I've got two copies, so sign both."

After Richard signed, Jack handed them to me. "You sign too, Jonnie, just here. Now, Dick, give Jonnie your AMEX. When that's processed, I'll sign these documents."

When Richard handed me the card, our eyes briefly met. I thought they'd be remorseful or pitiful, but they weren't; they were full of hatred. It shocked me. He was the one who had committed the crimes, abused my goodwill and trust and yet he was full of hatred. I ran the card for a total of $122,720, including the 4% card fee. I'd never put through such a huge amount before. I was willing to bet that I'd beaten Joe's sales that day and all from one appointment.

Sure enough, Richard got a call from AMEX. He confirmed the transaction and hung up.

Jack fired up again, "Right, Dick, you have until 5pm today to get the details of all clients to Jonnie. Jonnie's team will send the letters out to the clients stating they have acquired each of your firms. You can draft your own letter if you wish. If any clients call you, you are to refer them back to Jonnie. If we hear of any foul play, I'll press charges immediately. Understood?"

"You're enjoying this, aren't you?" Richard seethed to Jack.

"You bet I am." Jack smiled.

Richard stood and walked out the office, slamming the door.

I was exhausted.

Jack turned to me and smiled. "That was fun!"

"You're ruthless," I said. "I'm glad you're on my side." He shook my hand. "How did you know he had a Black AMEX?" I asked.

"Mike asked Sally how Joe and Richard claimed their travel expenses. They give her their credit card statements with the charges," he said.

I smiled. "Thanks, Jack. I don't know what to say. It's a lot to process."

"I know. And my pleasure. You're a good man, Jonnie and good guys often get taken advantage of. So, this was a win for the good guys."

A win for the champions, I thought.

After Jack left, I called Sally, Joe and Drew into the office and told them everything. Sally admitted she never liked him. And she was curious what had happened, when he stormed out the office slamming the front door.

Joe put two and two together and realised he started losing clients soon after Richard started. Every big deal he closed, anything over $10,000, the next time he'd visited the client, he was undercut by one of Richard wholesales companies. He thought it was just tough competition, when all along, he was bidding against Richard.

After the team meeting, I called Mike on his cell phone. He picked up immediately.

"How did it go?' he said without saying hello.

"Jack nailed him, Mike. He's a machine."

"Yep, Jack the Ripper they call him. Doesn't just go for the juggler; he rips out their insides as well."

"No kidding."

"So, you flicked the dick and got some of your cash back," he said.

"Yeah. You were right about Richard. How did you know?"

"Experience. I've dealt with people like Richard before. First one made me bankrupt, ruining my first marriage. With the second one, I had Jack and took him to the cleaners."

"It's sad it happens so much," I said.

"I agree. But with the principles and experience you have now, it won't happen again. You'll spot losers and vampires faster. They'll hardly have time to make a scratch."

"Thanks again, Mike."

"Pleasure. A win for the team. Talk to you next week."

"Yep."

What a day. I had a wholesale job to print that night. Richard made me sign wholesale agreements with *his* companies, stating I was not permitted to directly contact the end-client in anyway. Now

I know why he was so pedantic about it. But I legally owned these clients now.

I called them up and told the owners I'd just acquired the printing company they usually dealt with, skipping the details of the Richard deal, but mentioning Richard's name. I discovered they had not yet paid for the job, which meant that payment was coming to me, along with it's 40% profit margin. I also found out it wasn't urgent (despite Richard telling me so); next week would be fine.

I called Drew into my office and asked if he wanted to do some overtime next week and get paid actual overtime rates. He jumped at the chance. So, I gave him the job to schedule.

I called my wife and told her to get a babysitter. I was taking her out on a date and I'd be home in an hour. I finished some paperwork, turned off my computer, walked out of the factory, said goodbye to Sally and left the office with the sun still in the sky. It was the first in a long time. I had almost forgotten what day-time looked like. I would actually get to see my kids before they went to bed.

WEEK 7

Since the Jack the Ripper meeting last Wednesday, I'd slept an average of 7 blissful hours per night. That was 42 hours in the last six days. The difference that made to my sense of being and attitude towards life was tremendous. I hadn't said fluffy-duck all week. I hadn't even had the need or desire to.

Life was wonderful.

I was feeling awake, well rested and looking forward to my call with Mike.

My phone buzzed. "Our saviour is on the line," Sally said.

"God bless, put him through."

"Mike!" I said it like a kid inside an ice cream factory.

"Jonnie, how's your week been?"

"Best in five years, thanks to you."

"Wonderful to hear."

"How about you, Mike? I never really ask about your week."

"Busy week. We closed a deal on Friday, so I'm happy about that. And we've ordered a fleet of new trucks for our southern hub."

"Wow. I'm curious Mike, how big was the deal?"

"Well, it's a $30 million contract, but that makes it sound bigger than it is because that's the full-term value, which is five years. The annual revenue is six million."

"Wow, that's great. How do you get used to those numbers?"

"Well, it's like anything: once you become familiar with it, it's just another deal. What's important is whether there's profit in it, as you know and whether the team can deliver. Doesn't matter how big that number is; without profit and delivery, it's worthless."

"Yeah, you should be proud. I'm proud of you. That's an amazing business you've built."

"Thanks, Jonnie. You too. You've hung in there, that's the tough part. Now let's see if we can make it even better."

"Alright, well, I've got my notebook open to a clean page."

"Great. Business is like the Olympics."

"We've left the garden then?"

"Yep, it's weed-free, so we're done with that."

"I see, makes sense."

"What does the winner get at the Olympics?" he asked.

"Gold," I said.

"Yep."

"I hope you don't expect me to give my staff gold."

"No, something much more valuable than that."

"What? Plutonium?"

Mike laughed. "No, even more valuable than that."

"Really, what?"

"Recognition."

"Seriously?"

"You've got kids. What do they want more than anything?"

"Ice cream," I said.

"You mean they don't clamour for your attention? Want to show you things?" he asked.

I hadn't really thought about it like that. But now that he mentioned it, my kids were always trying to get my attention. *Look at this, Daddy; look what I can do, Daddy! Will you play with me, Daddy?*

"Yeah, you're right," I said.

"We all want attention. And your team is no different. But in the working environment, the best attention you can give them is recognition of a job well done. That's why we have this business principle: Always reward the champions."

I wrote it down in my notebook.

Always reward the champions.

"Now, you have your stats, so it's easy to see who the champions are. The ones with rising graphs, the ones who make their quotas," Mike said.

"So, we're talking about bonuses."

"Not necessarily. Bonuses are good and you should pay them, but recognition is more than just money. At your weekly staff meeting, when you review the statistics with your team, make a point of really acknowledging those who did a good job, those with improved stats. That is priceless."

"Am I meant to be holding a weekly meeting with my staff?" I asked.

"Yes. Absolutely. The purpose of the meeting is to review the weekly stats and to set quotas for the following week."

I made a note in my book.

"It's a quick meeting. No long discussions. Just review stats, reward the champions, plan for the coming week. That's it."

I made a note. We should do this on Friday afternoons, I thought, at the end of the week.

Mike continued, "To give you some ideas, we reward our team in lots of ways. We have trophies for the best sales, biggest deals, highest ever; one's called the rocket—that's someone whose stats have taken off vertically like a rocket. We've got lots of rewards. Each person gets a little prize, like movie tickets, dinner at a fine restaurant, opera tickets, trips to theme parks—all sorts."

"Wow, that's cool."

"Yeah, the team loves it. It's amazing what they'll do to get the reward. They get bonuses too, each quarter, but you know, I rarely hear about them. What they talk about are the trophies and the experiences. We even surveyed the team and discovered, while they like the bonuses, it's the rewards that motivate them."

"How interesting. I wonder what rewards I should do for my team," I said.

"Don't guess; ask them. In your meeting this week, get them all to write down what they want as a reward. You decide what gets rewarded, such as sales, etc., but let the team tell you what rewards they want."

"OK, great."

"Now, here's a tip. You might have more than one person win the reward each week. For example, if you set your individual quotas and everyone makes their quota, you reward everyone. No favorites, no competition. If they are all champions, reward them all."

"OK, makes sense. And what about bonuses?"

"The best way to do that is work out your breakeven; anything above that, allocate a percentage to a bonus pool that is shared with the whole team. Managers and those with more responsibility get a bigger stake of the pool. For example, for every $2 a manager receives, their juniors would get $1 or something like that. I recommend you do this every quarter; otherwise, it's too much admin work. Follow?"

"Yes," I said, as I madly scribbled notes.

"Now, your sales team need to have a sales bonus as well as a team bonus. Again, work out a breakeven or minimum amount. We base the minimum on at least three-times their salary. So, if they cost us say $100,000 per year, including benefits, then we'll expect them to sell at least $300,000; anything above that and we pay a bonus."

"Right, how much bonus?"

"Depends on your business. Anywhere from half a percent up to 2% of the revenue collected. You can also give them a surprise bonus too, if they close an amazing deal. But, it's good to have a structured approach."

"Great, Joe will love this."

"Well, that's all, Jonnie. I gotta fly."

"Thanks, Mike, talk next week."

I buzzed Sally. "Hey, Sally."

""Yes?" she said.

"We're going to have a team meeting every Friday at 4.30pm. I want you to make sure we have all the stats for the week up to date so we can review them as a team."

"OK, everyone needs to attend?" she asked.

"Yes, the whole team," I said.

"What about coffee and cake?"

"Sure, why not." I clicked off.

Now, I needed to meet with Joe, so we could work out his bonuses together. I sent him a text.

"Hey Joe when will you be in the office next?"

"This afternoon around 4."

"Great. Need to meet to discuss bonuses. Just got a plan from Mike."

"OK great! See you then."

Right, what stats should we reward?

Joe arrive just after 4 p.m. He popped his head in my office, "Er ... John, I want to get these orders written up and get them to Drew, that way we'll get the delivery stats up. Can we meet after?"

"Of course, no problem, just come back when you're ready." Amazing. He'd been waiting for bonuses for five years and postponed the meeting to get the stats up. What a champion.

Shortly after five, he knocked on the door again.

"Come in, Joe. How'd you do today?"

"Great, averaged $620 per order," he said proudly.

"You love beating that stat!"

"It's so simple, I can't believe I never looked at it before. I was always trying to beat the Dick and go for a big order. Now, I look at every client as a $500 sale. I start there and before I know it, they're ordering more."

Poor Richard. He was now called the Dick by everyone in the office.

"That's brilliant," I said. "So listen, here's how Mike works his bonuses."

I went over the details, his salary and the cost of the business. We agreed on a sliding scale. He'd get 1% for sales above $180k per year. Plus, another 1% bonus for everything above $500k. He was on track to getting close to a $10k bonus over the next 12 months, but I silently planned to give him more if he did a million. We also discussed hiring more salespeople and him becoming the sales manager. He admitted that he might not be management material and I admitted that neither was I. We both laughed.

For our first inaugural weekly meeting, I bought several trophies, a bunch of movie tickets, vouchers to a local fancy restaurant and a trumpet. It was a covert operation that I did, even without Sally finding out.

The trumpet, of course, was to announce the start of the meeting. I gave it a loud toot. It was corny, but it made them all smile.

I looked around at my team all squashed in our tiny boardroom, with Sally in her pink blouse on my left, Joe in his white shirt and pocket-pens on my right, Drew next to him and our two junior printers, Todd and Steve at the other end of the table.

After the trumpet blow, I announced, in an overly official voice, "The first inaugural weekly meeting has commenced."

Then I sat down and began, "OK team, so the purpose—"

Drew interrupted, "I think you should do the whole meeting in that fancy voice."

"Me too," said Sally.

"Agreed," said Steve.

I looked at Joe. "Are you going to join in this mutiny?" I asked.

"It was quite impressive," he said.

"I don't think I can," I admitted. "Alright, so the purpose of this meeting is to review the week's stats, reward the champions and plan for next week. I want it to be quick, then we can all go home."

They all appeared attentive, so I clicked the TV remote and fired up the flatscreen on the wall. Sally had already brought up the stats on MetaPulse. We went through each stat, most of which were up. Here's what they looked like:

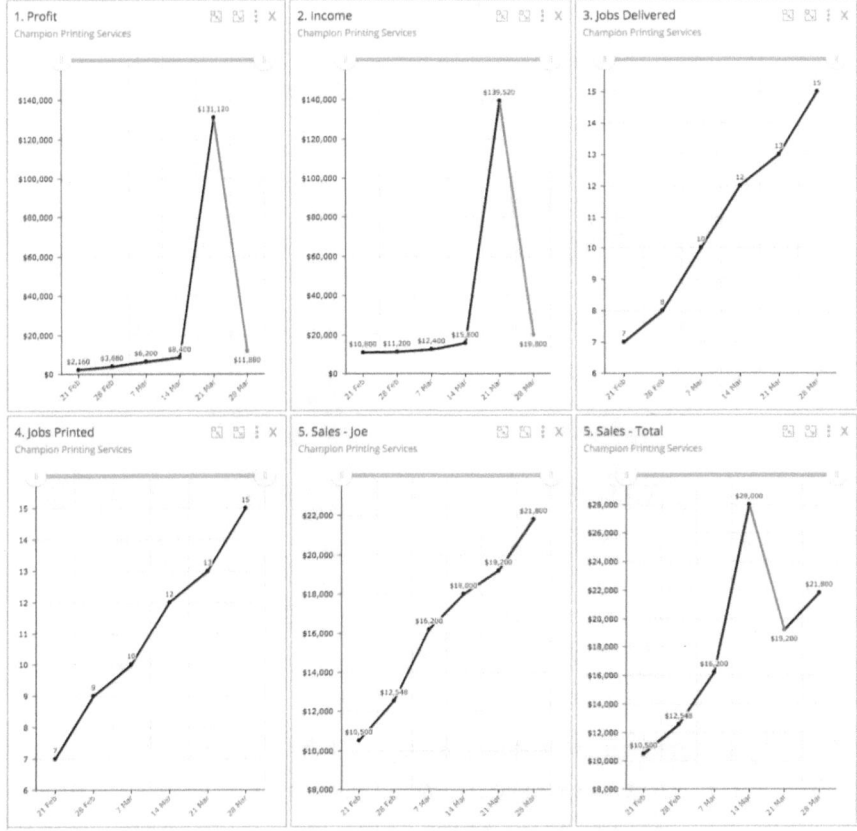

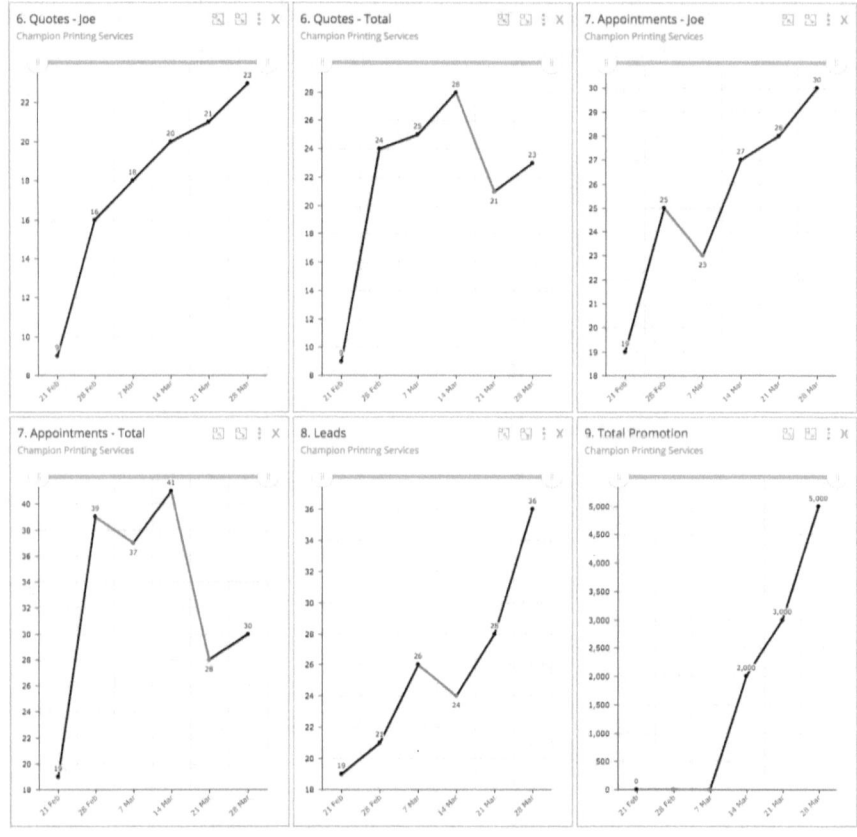

Everyone had made their quotas, so I handed out five trophies. Sally got the dinner tickets, because she loves eating out. The rest got movie tickets. With Sally being the only female on the team, the boys joked that she was being favored because she got the fancy restaurant tickets. I told them it was a bonus for putting up with me, which they all thought was fair enough.

I then asked them what kinds of rewards they wanted and to write them down.

We then worked out the quotas for next week. At Sally's request, I was also given a sales quota. We'd received a few phone calls from clients of the Dick and with Joe already being so busy, I was the new sales guy. Having being cooped up in the office for so long, I was looking forward to it.

The meeting went a bit longer because nobody left. We chatted away and I couldn't help but feel proud. These guys were like an extended family.

When everyone left, I reviewed the list of requested rewards:

Movie tickets
Go-karting
Sky dying
Bungee jumping
Dirt bike riding
iTunes vouchers
Concert tickets (unless it's *Queen*, ha ha)
Fancy restaurants

Todd and Steve had pretty much the same list and they were obviously the adventurous type. The *Queen* reference was from Steve. I figured I'd get him tickets to the opera as payback. The fancy restaurants were Sally's idea. I couldn't imagine her dirt bike riding; she'd ruin her pink blouse.

WEEK 8

"Morning, Mike!" I said like a kid who owned an ice cream shop.

"Morning, Jonnie. How'd your weekly meeting go?"

"Great, the team loved it. I've got a list of rewards and they're all geared up to meet their quotas this week."

"Brilliant. Well, I've got one more principle for you."

"Really, you mean this is the last one?"

"Not exactly, but it's the last one for now. Once you expand and grow more, we'll cover the others."

"But we'll still chat each week, though, right?" I asked concerned. Mike was my rock; I loved our weekly chats.

"Of course."

I was relieved. "So, what's business like this week?" I asked.

"Business is like a first date."

"Oh, we're getting kinky?"

"Not that part of the date," he said.

"Bummer."

"When people are on a first date, how do they treat each other?"

"Well ... they're courteous and polite and they listen."

"True, but the essence of what they do is to deliver on a promise and then some. They turn up on time or early. They might bring a gift. They go out of their way to make sure the other person is happy and impressed. That is how you need to treat your clients."

"You want me to date my clients?"

He laughed. "No Jonnie, but you need to treat them well."

"Right, well, that's a relief, because I don't think my wife would be too pleased. So, is that the rule? Treat them well?"

"The rule is: Always deliver what you promise and then some."

I wrote it down.

Always deliver what you promise and then some.

Mike continued, "For example, if you say a job will be ready in two days, don't take three days; do it in two days or better still, do it in less than two days."

"Makes sense."

"But, then do something a little extra."

"You mean like something for free?" I asked.

"Maybe or something they need."

"Free pens or something?"

"Yeah," he paused. "How many clients print something with a spelling mistake?"

"Happens all the time," I said.

"Well, what if you found the mistake for them and pointed it out before you printed it. That's going that extra mile; it shows you care. It's like opening the car door on date night."

"I see. Sometimes we do that, but that's only if we pick it up. I could get Sally to check over each job before we print it. She's great at finding typos."

"There you go. It's the little things that make the difference. You'd be surprised at what a difference it makes. This is the key to word-of-mouth marketing. Don't just do a good job; do an amazing job."

"I like it."

"Well, that's all for this week."

"Perfect, thanks, Mike. So, we're still on for next week?"

"Yes, but from here on, there are no more principles until you grow or until you run into problems. You have everything you need to build a great business, just keep getting the stats up, promote more, sell more, deliver more and reward your team. Rinse and repeat. That's the formula."

"It sounds so simple, Mike."
"It is. Only guys like Richard make it hard."
"True. OK, talk next week."

I liked the idea of checking for typos. I wondered what else we could do? I bet Sally and Joe had some ideas.

WEEK 20 (3 months later)

I have a problem. But it's a good problem.

Over the past 3 months, we'd broken all previous records, every single week. We'd got a new, young receptionist named Jessica and we moved Sally to the role of office manager.

We added two additional members to the sales team. One is a working-mom called Sharon, who starts work at 10 and finishes at 3 so she can get the kids to and from school. Even so, she was already selling above her $5,000 weekly quota. The other recruit is Sam, he's a young gun, super enthusiastic. He cracked $10k last week. Plus he loves *Queen*, so he's my new favorite. But don't tell Sally.

As a side note, recruiting people was a lot easier than before. I showed potential recruits the stats and how we worked with daily reporting and weekly quotas. Sharon and Sam both got really excited in their interviews when I covered this point. A couple of others I interviewed showed little interest; one yawned and another checked his phone. Neither bothered calling back to see if they got the job, yet both Sharon and Sam sent me several text messages, saying how they loved our culture and really wanted the job. I could immediately see, from the reactions of the potential recruits, who was likely to be a champion and who wasn't.

Joe is now officially sales manager. We re-worked his bonuses, so he gets a cut of the team, but he's still managing to keep his own stats up. He's picked up the big deals from the Dick's clients and his appointment average is through the roof. A few weeks ago, he closed a $25,000 deal from one appointment. For that, I created a new trophy:

Biggest Deal of the Month. It's a massive trophy that sits in the middle of the trophy cabinet, now located in the reception area. Joe was the first to get his name engraved on it, but Sharon has threatened to unseat him this month.

Drew's team has also grown. We've now got a second lead technician, Jamie, who clocks on just before Drew clocks off. Jamie works the late afternoon to evening shift, running Betty until 12pm. That's doubled our capacity, but we're still not keeping up.

And that's my problem. We're selling too much!

I need to get another printing machine, like Betty, but they cost a fortune. Plus, I don't really have the room. I've been looking at second-hand machines, because they are more affordable, but it's still a stretch.

That's what I'm going to ask Mike today; he should call any moment.

Our weekly calls have mostly been updates and lots of banter. No new business principles, just reiterating the same ones. Still, they have been priceless. I'm working on a gift for Mike, a way of saying thanks for all his help. But I need to find out something first.

My phone buzzed. "Our knight in shining armour for you," Sally said.

"Mike!" I said, like a kid who needed to buy an ice cream factory.

"Jonnie, how was your week?"

"Another highest ever across the boards," I bragged.

"I think I should invest in your business."

"Too late, you can't afford it," I teased.

"Maybe you should start giving me advice."

"You couldn't afford that either."

"Tough negotiator."

"But I do have one problem."

"Oh, you need my advice. I think I'll have to charge you."

"But it's your fault I have this problem."

"Well, in that case, it's on the house. What's up?"

"We're selling too much. I can't keep up delivery, even with Jamie working the late shift. I could try hiring another tech, but finding one willing to work from midnight to 7 a.m. will be tough. He'd have to be a vampire."

"Yeah, we don't want those; you just got rid of one," he said.

"Exactly. I've looked at buying another machine, like Betty, but it's so expensive; even second-hand ones cost a lot."

"I think it's time for the next business principle."

"Really? Wow. Have I just achieved some major milestone?"

"Yes."

"What is it?"

"Expansion problems."

"Oh, cool. Do I get a trophy?"

"I'll see what I can arrange," he said.

"Can't wait. I've got my notebook open; hit me with it."

"Business is like fishing."

"No more date night?"

"They don't mix well," he said.

"Agreed, so fishing?"

"What's the difference between the size of fish the guy caught and the size of fish he tells you he caught?" he asked.

"The latter is always bigger?" I said.

"Correct. And that is the best way to tackle your business problems."

"Lie about them?" I asked.

"No, make them bigger."

"Huh? You lost me."

"Here's the rule: Always tackle a tough problem by making the problem bigger."

I wrote it in my book.

> Always tackle a tough problem
> by making the problem bigger.

"A few years ago, we had a similar problem to you. Our fleet was at maximum capacity and I needed to buy about ten new trucks. Like you, I was looking to do it as cheaply as possible. At the time, our fleet was a mixture of old and new, different models and brands. They all had different maintenance schedules. Then, I had a bright idea. Instead of negotiating ten trucks, I wondered what kind of deal I could get with a hundred and ten. I made the problem bigger."

"Wow! But that would have cost a fortune."

"You'd think so, but actually not. You see, in the deal, we negotiated a maintenance contract. Every model was the same, so that saved us a fortune in repairs. Also, we sold all the other vehicles in our fleet. The annual cost worked out better than buying ten trucks. And, of course, with an entirely new fleet, delivery issues due to breakdown dropped to zero."

"Amazing." My mind was churning. How could I apply this idea? But Mike answered the question for me.

"So, instead of buying one second-hand machine, Jonnie, why not by three new ones?"

"That's a scary thought."

"But you don't know the numbers. Plus, I bet a new machine is faster, can print more and being new it will give you less troubles."

"You're right. I could sell Betty and the other smaller printers I have. That will give me extra room too. I might be able to fit 3 of the newer models in the factory; they're more compact than Betty."

"Well, it's time to find out. With that kind of printing power, you could easily 5X your business."

"Awesome, Mike. I'm going to make a few calls and see who can give me the best deal."

"Great. Have a good week."

"You too. Oh, quick question. Does your wife like *Queen*?"

"She's not really a fan, why?"

"Mine either. Just wondering."

"OK, see ya."

Three new printers? That was about $1.5 million in new assets. But I wondered what the overall cost was? It was time to find out.

The following week, I got a package in the mail. A trophy. It must have been custom-made because the guy on it was in that tell-tail Freddie Mercury pose, with his legs apart, one hand in the air, with a clenched fist. The inscription read:

Jonnie Maine
Expansion Extraordinaire.

What a legend. I put it on the bench, just under my shrine of *Queen*.

WEEK 24 (4 weeks later)

It's 6 p.m. on Thursday night. I'm still in the office, although this is late for me nowadays, as I'm usually gone by five, but everyone works late on Thursdays. We made Thursday the last day of the week. We had to because no one wanted to come to the weekly meetings on Friday; they were more interested in getting their stats up. So, Friday is the start of the week and we review the stats from Friday to Thursday. That's why everyone works later on Thursday; it's their last chance to beat their weekly quotas. The team stays back closing deals, printing jobs, collecting money. Sally makes the couriers come later and bribes them with beer and chocolates. The beer seems to work better.

Over the past four weeks, I've been knee-deep in sales reps and brochures—buying 1.5 million dollars worth of machines is hard work! Especially when you've got three different companies all vying for the deal.

I've been working with Drew on this project because, as lead technician, I want him to be happy with the machines we get. He's got loads of experience running machines, more than me. The important aspects of the deal are price, maintenance contract and training. These machines are computerised, so there's a steep learning curve for the guys. The key to the deal is selling Betty and the other machines. One of the companies gave me the name of a second-hand dealer who's coming to look at them today.

But overall, with the leasing contract and savings, it's affordable. We can expand our services and improve our delivery times. I never would have even dreamed of this. And to think, just a few months ago, I could hardly pay the rent.

WEEK 28 (4 weeks later)

After long deliberation, Drew and I agreed on the printers we wanted. We waited until we sold Betty; otherwise, I'd have nowhere to put her—plus, I needed the cash because I was not only buying three new machines, I was hiring three new technicians as well.

So here I was, with Drew, on a Saturday, watching a team of guys lift Betty onto a flatbed truck. They had to take part of the roof off for the crane cable.

I know it sounds silly, but I was feeling a little nostalgic. Watching Betty swinging helplessly in the air, I felt like a family member was leaving. I'd spent so many hours with her, watching her hum away, fixing her, cleaning her. Heck, I think I spent more nights with her than with my wife.

With Betty out of the factory, the place looked huge. And barren. My stomach did a somersault at the idea of the new machines being late.

Drew and I spent the rest of the day cleaning up and arranging the space for the new machines, which were planned for delivery tomorrow.

I was at the office again, on a Sunday, but I wasn't alone. I had the family with me. Tiffany had baked a cake, with the Champion Printers' logo on it and three candles. Drew was there of course, overseeing things. Sally and Joe turned up with their spouses. Sarah was there too with her husband and kids. Even Sam, with his girlfriend, Jessica with her boyfriend and Jamie the new tech. My folks turned up too. Steve and Todd were manning the BBQ. It was a real family affair. I had *Queen* playing in the background.

When the trucks arrived, everyone cheered. Drew and I had marked out the floor exactly where we wanted each printer. The installation was surprisingly fast; the machines were so compact and sleek. It was like getting a new smartphone, only bigger and a lot more expensive.

After the install guys had left, we held an official naming ceremony. I blew my trumpet for attention and named each machine. I didn't think smashing a bottle of champagne against them was a good idea. Instead, we had special name plaques made up, which I attached. One was named *Nelson*, the other *Mandela* and the last was, of course, *Queen Machine*.

Then the team got together and said they had a present for me. But first, I was blindfolded. Then I heard one of the printing machines fire up; someone was using *Mandela*. It had to be Drew because he'd been in training and vividly reading the manuals over the past few weeks.

"You'd better not be trying to steal that machine," I joked. "I know where you live."

After several minutes and a very quiet hum, I heard a few of them go "Ahh…"

Tiffany took off my blindfold; Joe and Drew were holding a poster. It was the first thing ever printed with our new machines. It was a picture of Mandela, with a quote:

> *A good head and a good heart are always*
> *a formidable combination.*

"To Jonnie," Sally said holding up a glass, "our champion."
"To Jonnie," the team joined in.
I was speechless. And that damn dust got in my eyes again.

WEEK 32 (4 weeks later)

Tuesday morning, 7.55 a.m. Almost Mike time. I was sitting at my desk, dumbfounded.

I was playing with MetaPulse and used a feature that allows you to change the frequency of the graphs. You can make them daily, weekly, monthly or yearly.

We always use weekly stats, but we'd just started a new month, so I flicked it over to monthly out of curiosity. I couldn't believe it.

Joe, Sarah and Sam had collectively sold over $250,000 worth of printing last month. Prior to Mike's help, that took half a year to achieve and we'd done it in one month. I'd been so focused on the week-by-week progress that it hadn't dawned on me just how far we'd come.

At that rate, it meant I had a business with an annual revenue of three million, six times what it was when I started. And we weren't even at full capacity yet with our new machines.

My phone buzzed. "Magic Mike for you," Sally said.

"Mike!" I said like a kid with a triple ice cream cone.

"Jonnie, good week?"

"Mike, I was just looking at MetaPulse and last month, we did a quarter of a million. I can't believe it."

He was quiet.

"Mike?"

"Well done, buddy. Really. Brilliant result."

"Couldn't have done it with you."

"Your win is my win, Jonnie. It's been fun sharing this journey with you. I think you're ready for the next lesson."

"There's more?"

"Two more."

"Really, OK, let me turn to a new page."

"I'm going to give you both of them."

"Two in one phone call? Does that cost more?" I asked.

"Twice as much as usual."

"Expensive."

"You can afford it now."

"True. So, hit me."

"Business is like a good joke."

"My business was a joke until you showed up."

He laughed. "Like all good jokes, they're more enjoyable when shared with others. Here's the rule: Always share your success with your community; give back."

I wrote it in my notebook.

> Always share your success with
> your community; give back.

He continued, "We sponsor schools and charities. Last year, we helped fund a new hospital wing. Helping like that provides a feeling of joy and pride no balance sheet will ever give you. And when you do, it comes back in waves."

"I love it, Mike."

"I knew you would," he said. "We set aside a percentage of profits every quarter. We have regular funding programs we sponsor during the year, but we build up a nest-egg and do something big once a year. We set our quotas against it too and the whole team gets involved. The guys on the trucks know, while they're driving late at night, they too help build a hospital wing. It gives them a sense of pride no amount of money can buy. Whenever we get recognition, I always make sure it's *The Team at Salsbury Freight* on the plaque."

"Perfect. I've got just the thing to get started on too."

"Wonderful. And here's the next and final principle."

I turned to a new page in my book.

"Business is a game. When you know how to win the game, write down what you know so others can play and win too. That other notebook I told you to get, at the very start, it's where you keep track of all of your successful actions and the things that worked. That book is how you play the game and win. You need to make sure your whole team knows those rules. Get your team to write down how they play and win. When you've done that, you'll have a game plan for the entire business, where anyone can join and everyone can win."

"You're a genius."

"I know."

"And modest."

"I know."

"So, what's this last rule: Play to win?" I asked.

"No, it's more than that. It's this: When you know how to win the game, share what you know so others can win too."

I wrote it in my notebook:

> When you know how to win the game,
> share what you know so others can win too.

"The team is going to love that one," I said.

"No doubt."

"So, even though you've shared with me all the business principles, I'd still like to chat every Tuesday. I love our chats; I get so many ideas."

"I enjoy it too. Besides, I can't think of anything better to do on Tuesdays at 8 in the morning."

"I'm flattered," I said.

That gave me an idea; I bet other business people would love to meet up and have someone to talk to.

"OK, Jonnie, got fly. Talk next week," he said.

"Thanks, Mike."

In the weekly meeting with the team, I shared Mike's last two business principles, which by the way, I now call the *Champion Principles*.

We all wrote down how each of us plays the game of business. Everyone had a notebook and jotted down what works for them. We called them our *Play to Win* books. Sally said she'd type them up and put them in a file: the *Play to Win* file.

I set up a new bank account purely for charity and worked out a percentage of quarterly profits we could comfortably allocate. I wanted to do something useful for the community, like Mike, so I intended to let the amount build up.

I did, however, make a small contribution. Our first charity donation was new uniforms and equipment for my son's baseball team. The coach suggested we put the logo on the t-shirt, but then it wouldn't be charity; that's sponsorship. I was so proud watching the game and seeing the boys in their new outfits and equipment.

WEEK 52

My idea of helping local business owners has taken off. Every Wednesday, we host a breakfast workshop. We call it our *Champion Workshop*. It's free.

The first time we held it, only 3 people turned up. I showed them our stats on MetaPulse and covered *Champion Principle #1*. The following week, those three brought three more. It got so popular, we moved it into the factory. At the rate it's going, I'll have to buy a new building just for the meetings.

Joe and Sam attend and always come away with orders. I started with the idea to give back, but so far, it's given us more.

For our annual community project, Sally suggested that we offer to renovate an old people's home that's a few blocks from our office. Her father resides there and the place is old and dismal. We paid a visit together and looked around. It was pretty bleak. We got some contractors in to quote on the work and it will cost about two-hundred thousand. Per my projections, that will take us about 18 months to raise. When I mentioned it to Mike, he said, "I'll throw in half." What a champion! That brought it much closer.

I reviewed the stats and worked out a plan to reduce the time to 6 months. We took the entire team on a tour of the home and then came back to the office. I showed them the quotas of what we needed to do to make the money in 6 months.

They blitzed it. We did it in four.

Renovations start next week. Sally volunteered to be project manager. I pity those workers. She's already worked out what stats they need to report to her daily. Got it set up in MetaPulse, ready to go.

I was finally able to get the perfect gift for Mike. I knew what I wanted and one day, I finally found it: A *Queen* tribute band playing in Las Vegas. I bought two seats, front row center. Plus, a nice suite in the hotel for him. I mailed him his ticket, attached to a picture of Mandela with the following quote:

It always seems impossible until it's done.

It was Tuesday, 7.59 a.m., a year since my first phone call where Mike began sharing his wisdom. If anyone had told me what I'd accomplish in one year, I would have said it was impossible. But is wasn't. It was done.

My phone buzzed. "Archangel on the phone for you," said Sally.

"Mike!"

"Jonnie, I just got your gift. I haven't been to a concert in years! You're coming too, right?"

"Of course, got the seat right next to you."

"How you getting there?"

"I'm catching a flight in the morning. I'll arrive early in the afternoon."

"Like hell you will. I'll come get you in the Gulfstream."

Awesome, I thought, but I played it cool. "That'll be great."

"I see you got me a room too. You staying in the same hotel?"

"Yeah."

"Listen, how about I upgrade us to the penthouse suite; it has two or three bedrooms, I can't remember. You bring your missus and I'll bring mine. They can enjoy a pampering, while we enjoy some Queen."

"That's a great idea."

"And don't worry, I'll cover the extra costs."

"This was my attempt to buy you a gift," I said.

"I know and I love it. But when you give, you get more back."

"I've noticed that."

"I'm looking forward to this. Only two weeks!" he said like a kid in an ice cream shop.

"Me too. I've heard the band is great; they even look like them."

We bantered more about business and things and then hung up.

WEEK 54

Mike's plane arrived on the tarmac and taxied slowly to a stop. Tiffany was more excited than me, hopping from one foot to the next. She was acting like a kid in an ice cream shop. It was becoming a pandemic.

When the steps unfolded, Mike appeared at the door and waved us over. He came to greet us, embracing Tiffany first and then giving me a big bear hug. Mike had always been bigger than me and I was engulfed in his arms.

"You look great, Jonnie."

"You too, Mike."

"Please," he pointed to the stairs.

Mike's wife, Rebecca, greeted us as we entered and took our coats, despite there being a hostess. Mike gestured to the seats, two on either side of the aisle facing each other with tables in between. The plane was covered in cream leather and mahogany wood. I'd have to 10X my business to afford something like this, but that idea didn't seem like such an impossible feat. Give it time, I thought.

The flight was smooth. We had so much to talk about. I was so engrossed in our conversation that I forgot we were on a plane.

Mike had a limo waiting for us at the airport. Tiffany kept squeezing my hand in delight. The penthouse suite was like the plane, only bigger. It was on the top floor, so the view was about the same. While Rebecca and Tiffany surveyed the list of pamperings they would order after dinner, Mike handed me a wrapped gift.

I ripped it open. It was a *Queen* t-shirt and two wrist-sweatbands, so I could dress like the drummer. The t-shirt was exactly the same one we used to wear while jamming in his room, in the sixth grade.

"Where did you find these?"

"I didn't. I found an old picture of us and gave it to my assistant and asked her to find them. Took her two days."

"That's cheating."

Sometime later, the ladies exited their respective bedrooms, all dressed up for a fancy dinner. In contrast, Mike and I were wearing black t-shirts, denim jeans and I had my sweatbands on.

"Look at those two," said Rebecca, "like a couple of teenagers."

We all laughed.

I'd bought VIP tickets, which included pre-show drinks. But everywhere we went, we got the royal treatment. I think it's because we were staying in the penthouse. We were even ushered to our seats by security, just before the concert started.

When the band began to play, the crowd went wild and jumped to its feet, including Mike and me. We sang along to every song.

When *"We Are the Champions"* started, we put an arm around each other and sang at the top of our lungs.

I briefly thought about Richard and felt pity for him. I doubted he'd ever experienced friendship and camaraderie like this. My thoughts passed to my team. My team of champions.

As Mike and I swayed to the music, singing completely off-tune, I realized that despite our different businesses and their different sizes, we were the same. We were business owners. The whole world-wide economy is built on the business owner, with their Sallys, Joes and Drews. I realized that the business owner really is the champion of the world.

A Final Word, from Tony

I truly hope you enjoyed this book. I wrote it to be funny, entertaining and straight to the point, in the hope that you can quickly see the power of these simple principles and put them to work in your business.

The story, although made up, is nevertheless based on truth. Each character is the culmination of real-life people.

Jonnie, our hero, is the sum of all the champion business owners I've ever met. Often naive and full of enthusiasm, but unfortunately, just as often, overworked, underpaid, struggling and stressed, with an inner-guilt that they're neglecting family and friends. I see these people every day. I see one in the mirror every morning, although he's a little wiser now.

Richard is also an embodiment of the champion killers I've met along my business travels. You might think I embellished his character, making him appear more sly and cunning for effect. The truth is, Richard is quite mild. I've experienced first hand employees stealing and business partners lying and cheating. I've witnessed friends and clients suffer from the embezzlement of millions and sly business dealings that resulted in bankruptcy. While I don't wish to harp on this subject too much, I do want to impress upon you that champion killers exist. The damage they cause and the premeditated evil they are capable of is never truly appreciated until you witness it first hand.

It's hard to comprehend that a person can spend so much time (practically all their time) working on another's demise. A champion is so focused on winning and helping others that he never sees the bullets coming. He doesn't even own a gun. It's also why I'm sharing these insights with you, so you don't think it's all fiction. Hopefully, you can learn from this book, rather than from a real-life experience.

But if you've already had the unfortunate luck to have a champion killer in your midst, then you know what it's like. While you have every right to be bitter and resentful, it serves no purpose. It kills the *champion spirit* and in doing so it means the bad guys win. The best response is to rise again and to be successful. That's the ultimate revenge. Just like Jonnie and Nelson Mandela!

Thankfully, the champion killers are the minority, but they create the majority of problems. It's the 80/20 rule that 80% of your troubles in business come from 20% of the people. The actual percentage is more like 90/10; the champion killers are less than 10% but they create 90% of the difficulties.

But on the flipside, most, if not all, of your results come from the champions. They are what to focus on.

I can't take all the credit for Mike's wisdom; he is the culmination of real-life mentors—wisdom I've gained from books and from firsthand experience working with other stellar champions.

Sally, Joe and Drew are shining examples of the champions I've had the pleasure of working with. Sally is like a lady who used to work for me, named Maria. She too used to boss me around, but all in the direction of getting the stats up.

Another thing I'd like to share, regarding the three types of people Mike mentions—the champions, the losers and the champion killers—is that they make up a kind of scale, with the champions at the top, the killers at the bottom and the losers in the middle. They don't all have the same force or power. While some killers can be utterly ruthless, others can be pathetically mild and border on just being a loser. Also, a loser can be a loser out of ignorance and bad experiences. A little training and encouragement can turn them into a champion. Such people have rarely been given a chance to shine, but in an environment designed for champions, they can rise again. You don't need to be soft with such people, but at the same time, you don't need to be a tyrant either. Everyone (except vampires) deserves a second chance and sometimes all a loser needs is a little compassion.

When a loser proves they can be a champion, you must forget they were ever a loser. Treat them based on the stats they have today, not those they had yesterday.

In case you are wondering, jamming to the music of *Queen*—that sparked the friendship of our heroes—was also how I first learned of the band. My neighbor, Martin, was a couple years older than me. He had his own stereo in his room with speakers the size of cabinets, along with a huge collection of vinyl records (it was the eighties!). He taught me how to play air guitar without missing a cord and he introduced me to *Pink Floyd, Van Halen* and *The Eagles*, but our favourite was always *Queen*. We use to make his mother berserk playing music too loud. Tragically, Martin never made it past the age of 27, but our brief childhood friendship left an indelible mark on my life. I'm sure he's still jamming away somewhere.

So, that's a little of the back story to the book. It's closer to truth than fiction.

I strongly suggest you implement Mike's words of wisdom. I'd loved to hear of your wins and successes, even any questions you may have. You can reach out to me via tonymelvin.com.

Also, be sure to check out MetaPulse. It was built by a good friend of mine, Mikel Lindsaar (a real genius). It's the best online app for stats.

As a final note, in case you're wondering, you *are* a champion. Only a champion would read this book from cover to cover. Now, it's time for *you* to rise.
I wish you tremendous success.

Tony Melvin

February, 2019
Florida, USA

P.S. If you enjoyed this book, please help spread the word and leave a positive review on Amazon.

The Champion Principles

Download a free copy from tonymelvin.com/champions

1. Always measure the important steps towards your desired outcome.
2. Always know your breakeven.
3. Always focus on what you can improve.
4. What worked before will work again.
5. Your business has no place for losers or champion killers. Kill them off quickly before they kill you.
6. Always reward the champions.
7. Always deliver what you promise and then some.
8. Always tackle a tough problem by making the problem bigger.
9. Always share your success with your community; give back.
10. When you know how to win the game, share what you know so others can win too.

Spread the Word & Connect with Tony

Connect with Tony and share your favorite quote and tag #RiseOfTheChampions

Facebook @TonyMelvin.Writer
Twitter @tonymelvin
Instagram @tonyonenonly

To send a message Tony,
visit tonymelvin.com

To order paperback copies direct from the publisher
visit tonymelvin.com/champions

MetaPulse for consultants

MetaPulse's Partner program is perfect for consultants.

Partners of MetaPulse have several benefits:

- Branded signup page with your own logo that automatically tracks your referrals.
- Ability to automatically add a predetermined series of graphs for your clients.
- Access to your client's statistics, so see their progress and effectively coach and mentor them.

To find out more visit metapulse.com/champions

With MetaPulse you can:

- Improve productivity
- Manage your business remotely
- Monitor the results of each team member
- Increase your sales and profits
- Have unlimited users
- Have unlimited teams
- Have unlimited companies

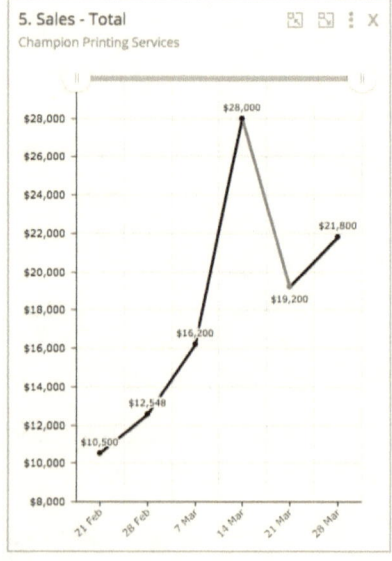

Start your 30-day free trial at metapulse.com/champions

Preloaded with the "stairway to profit" stats!

www.ingramcontent.com/pod-product-compliance
Lightning Source LLC
LaVergne TN
LVHW041648060526
838200LV00040B/1756